Practice Book

GRADE 2-2

Harcourt

Orlando Boston Dallas Chicago San Diego

Visit *The Learning Site!*
www.harcourtschool.com

Contents

Name _____

▶ **Finish the story. Write a word from the shirts on each line.**

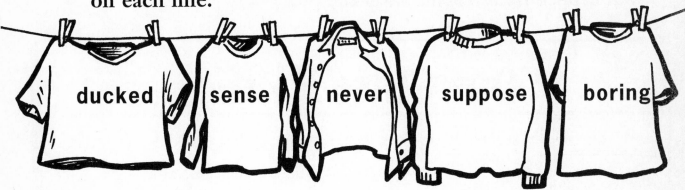

ducked   sense   never   suppose   boring

I _____ Grandpa lives in the best place in the

world. It's never _____ on his farm. One cold day I

_____ under the barnyard fence and saw all the animals

sleeping together. I had _____ seen anything so funny! I

guess it made _____ for the animals to sleep together to

keep warm.

Harcourt

TRY THIS! Write a story about your favorite farm animal. Use as many Vocabulary Words as you can.

SCHOOL-HOME CONNECTION Ask your child to make a list of the Vocabulary Words and then to read the words aloud to you. Then, talk about the meaning of each word.

Name _____

▶ **Read the newspaper beginning. Think about what will happen next. Then answer the questions.**

 # Our Class Picnic

Mrs. Day's second-grade class went on a picnic last Monday. We walked six blocks to the park. As we were walking, dark clouds filled the sky. When we reached the park, we heard thunder. We wished we could go indoors, but there was no place to go! Then we felt wet drops on our heads.

1. Will the class have the picnic? _____

2. Explain your answer. _____
What clues tell you what the weather was like?

3. _____

4. _____

5. _____

What clues tell you that the children couldn't keep dry by just running inside?

6. _____

7. _____

Harcourt

SCHOOL-HOME CONNECTION Work with your child to come up with the first part of a story about an unusual pet. Talk about what might happen at the end. Then ask your child to tell you an ending for the story.

Name _____

▶ **Read each pair of sentences. On the line next to the sentences, write who or what the underlined word stands for.**

1. We rode a bus on our school trip.
   It was shiny and new.   _____

2. Mr. Ray sat at the front. He said we
   were going to see wildflowers.   _____

3. There were so many flowers at the farm!
   They were red and yellow and blue.   _____

4. Mrs. Miller works there. She showed us
   around the farm.   _____

5. Mrs. Miller and Mr. Ray told us the
   names of all the flowers. They told us   _____
   not to pick any.   _____

6. I spotted the flower I liked best. It was
   beautiful and blue.   _____

7. Mrs. Miller liked that flower, too.
   She said it was a bluebonnet.   _____

8. Have you seen a bluebonnet? It is the
   state flower of Texas!   _____

Harcourt

TRY THIS! Look back at a story you have read. Find the word *she*, *he*, *they*, or *it*. Write who or what the word stands for in the sentence.

SCHOOL-HOME CONNECTION Work with your child to write a story about a class trip. Encourage him or her to use *she, he, it,* and *they* to refer to people and objects in the story.

Just in Time **7**

Name _____

▶ **Complete the sentences. Write each word in ( )
on the line where it belongs.**

We **(1)** _____ down the **(2)** _____ in our
car. **(road   rode)**

At last, we could **(3)** _____ the **(4)** _____.
(see   sea)

I couldn't **(5)** _____ to walk on the hot sand with my

(6) _____ feet. **(bare   bear)**

My sister **(7)** _____ the ball **(8)** _____
my sand pile. **(through   threw)**

Dad **(9)** _____ a prize after

swimming in just **(10)** _____
race. **(won   one)**

**TRY
THIS!** Think of two words that have different spellings but the same
sounds. Write a sentence for each word.

SCHOOL-HOME CONNECTION With your child, write a story about a
plain plane. Try to include other words that have the same sound but
different spellings and meanings, such as *bee* and *be* or *our* and *hour*.

Name _____

▶ **Finish each sentence. Write a pronoun from the box that can take the place of the noun in ( ). Remember to begin each sentence with a capital letter.**

I	you	he	she	they	it

1. _____ went to the farm. **(Max)**

2. _____ went, too. **(Liz)**

3. _____ saw many farm animals. **(the children)**

4. _____ were in the barn. **(the horses)**

5. _____ asked about the snake. **(Mr. Jung)**

6. _____ did not live on the farm. **(the snake)**

7. Mrs. Grant said, "_____ liked that snake."
(Mrs. Grant)

8. Mrs. Grant told Angie, "_____ would have liked it, too." **(Angie)**

Harcourt

TRY THIS! Draw a picture of something you and your friends like to do. Write two sentences to go with your picture. Use the pronouns *I* and *we* in your sentences.

SCHOOL-HOME CONNECTION Ask your child to tell you what a pronoun is. Then take turns saying sentences with the pronouns *I* and *you*.

Name _____

▶ **Complete the sentences. Write a Spelling
Word from the box on each line.**

pool	food	moon	root	tool	room

1. The _____ goes around the earth.

2. A _____ is the part of a
   plant that grows underground.

3. You can swim in the _____.

4. A _____ is something
   that helps you do a job.

5. _____ is something that you eat.

6. A _____ is part of a house.

Handwriting Tip: When you write
the letter *o* two times in a row, make
the letters stand apart from each other.

OO

▶ **On each line, write the Spelling Word again.**

7. noon _____   8. soon _____

9. cool _____   10. too _____

SCHOOL-HOME CONNECTION With your child, find objects
around your home that have the *oo* sound in their names,
such as *spoon*, *stool*, and *boots*. Spell the words aloud.

Harcourt

▶ **Solve the riddles. Write a word from the box on each line.**

vacation	relax	matador	captured
plains	manners	imagination	

1. He waves a cape. Who is he?

He's a ___matador___.

2. If you say "please," what do you have?

You have good ___manners___.

3. If you sit and rest, what do you do?

You ___relax___.

4. You won't see any hills here. Where are you?

You are on the ___plains___.

5. You go on this for fun. What is it?

It's a ___vacation___.

6. If you roped a cow, what did you do?

You ___captured___ it.

7. What do you use to think about new things?

You use your ___imagieation___.

SCHOOL-HOME CONNECTION With your child, make up a funny story about a vacation, using the vocabulary words. Ask your child to write a sentence about your story and to use at least one Vocabulary Word in the sentence.

Name _____

▶ **Solve the riddles. Write a word from the box
on each line.**

| toy | noise | cowboy | coin | boil | joy | soil | voice |

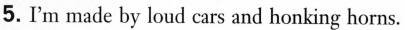

1. I work with cattle on the plains. Who am I? _____

2. I'm a penny or a dime. What am I? _____

3. I'm another word for *dirt*. What am I? _____

4. I'm what water does when you turn up the heat.

What am I? _____

5. I'm made by loud cars and honking horns.

What am I? _____

6. I'm another word for *happiness*.

What am I? _____

7. You use me when you talk.

What am I? _____

8. Children play with me.

What am I? _____

Harcourt

**TRY
THIS!** Write riddles like the ones on this page for the words *boy*
and *voice*.

SCHOOL-HOME CONNECTION Ask your child to write a sentence
about cowboys. Ask him or her to use at least one word that has the
same vowel sound as *toy*.

Name _____

▶ **Finish the story. On each line, write a word from the railroad track.**

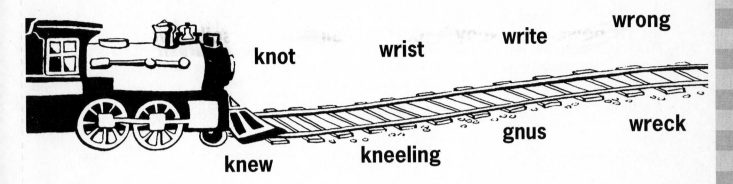

wrong

write

wrist

knot

gnus

wreck

kneeling

knew

I thought my vacation out West would be quiet, but I was

_____! On the very first day, I looked out the window

of the train and saw a herd of _____. One of them

was _____ right on the track! I _____

we had to stop fast, so I took action. I tied a _____ in

my rope and roped the animal's horn. Then I jerked my

_____ and pulled him out of the way. At the next

stop, newspaper people wanted to _____ stories about

me. They called me the hero who kept the train from having

a _____.

TRY THIS! Write a story about a train ride. Use at least one word that
has the letters *kn, gn,* or *wr.*

Harcourt

SCHOOL-HOME CONNECTION Ask your child to write a
funny poem about a gnat or a gnu.

Just in Time **13**

Name _____

▶ **Fill in the story path to show the order of events in "How I Spent My Summer Vacation."**

Wallace takes the train west.

Which part of the story do you like best? _____

_____

_____

SCHOOL-HOME CONNECTION Ask your child to tell you about the adventures Wallace has in the story "How I Spent My Summer Vacation."

Harcourt

Name _____

▶ **Read the story and look at the picture.**
Use clues in the story and the picture to figure
out what the underlined words mean. Then complete the
sentences. Write the correct word or words on each line.

Robin said, "I spent my summer vacation in the
desert. It was the most <u>arid</u> place I ever saw.
It hadn't rained there in years! I rode on a
<u>dromedary</u>. I had to sit on top of the big hump
on its back. That hump was <u>immense</u>! As the animal
<u>ambled</u> along, I swayed from side to side on its
back until I was <u>reeling</u> and dizzy. When I wanted to get off,
the camel had to kneel so I could <u>dismount</u>. I wish I could have
brought it home."

1. <u>Arid</u> means _____. **(rainy   dry   stormy)**

2. A <u>dromedary</u> is a _____. **(horse   donkey   camel)**

3. <u>Immense</u> means about the same as _____.
(enormous   tiny   tall)

4. <u>Ambled</u> means about the same as _____.
(walked   hopped   sang)

5. <u>Reeling</u> means about the same as _____.
(happy   fishing   dizzy)

6. To <u>dismount</u> means to _____.
(go around   ride across   get off)

SCHOOL-HOME CONNECTION Ask your child to read this
story to you. Then ask him or her to point out the sentence and
picture clues that make each underlined word's meaning clear.

Harcourt

Name _____

▶ **Use sentence clues to figure out what each underlined word means. Fill in the circle next to your choice.**

1 The fishers pushed the dory into the water and began to row.

A dory is a kind of _____.

⬭ plane

⬭ car

⬭ fish

⬭ boat

3 "Our little boat will never make it to shore in this squall. The wind is too strong!" I shouted through the rain.

A squall is a _____.

⬭ storm

⬭ lake

⬭ sunshine

⬭ yell

2 As I fished in the rain, I wore a mackintosh to keep dry.

A mackintosh is a _____.

⬭ belt

⬭ raincoat

⬭ ship

⬭ vest

4 "I'm going to spend my next vacation where the land is parched and it never rains," I said.

Parched means _____.

⬭ wet

⬭ dry

⬭ safe

⬭ cloudy

Harcourt

▶ **Complete the sentences. Write a word from the box on each line.**

action	decorations	invitation	nation
vacation	reflection	section	prediction

1. Daniel got an _____ to visit his uncle in San Antonio.

2. "Right now, I'll make a _____ that you'll love San Antonio," Uncle David said.

3. "We think our city is the most beautiful one in

the _____."

4. Daniel liked the _____ of town called Riverwalk.

5. People hung lights and other _____ outside their shops.

6. Daniel could see the _____ of the lights on the river.

7. "There's always some _____ here. It's never dull," said Uncle David.

8. "This is the perfect place for a _____!" Daniel said.

Harcourt

SCHOOL-HOME CONNECTION Ask your child to choose two words from the box. Then have him or her write two sentences using the words.

Name _____

▶ **Complete the rhymes. On each line, write a word from the box.**

| night | land | rope | west | team | hide | sticks |

1. Tip is my dog, and I think he's the best

Of all the cow dogs on the plains in the _____.

2. When Tip runs next to my horse as I ride,
Those cows that have wandered have no place to

_____.

3. My Tip doesn't do any plain old dog tricks,

Like walking on two legs or bringing back _____.

4. What Tip does is work like a real fine cowhand.

He goes after cows that have strayed off our _____.

5. He barks at those cows while I ride down the slope

And nips at their heels when I toss out my _____.

6. Then we lead them all back to our side of the stream.

Yes, Tip and I make such a wonderful _____!

7. We work through the day till we run out of light.
Then we head back to camp to bed down for the

_____.

SCHOOL-HOME CONNECTION With your child,
make a list of words that rhyme. Ask your child to
use some of the words in a poem.

Harcourt

Name _____

▶ **Read the words under each line. Choose the
describing word. Write it on the line.**

1. I am a _____ cowboy.
   (take tall talk)

2. I have a _____ hat.
   (big bark bus)

3. I wear _____ boots.
   (by black blow)

4. I ride a _____ horse.
   (bird brown build)

5. I have a _____ rope.
   (long lunch land)

6. I can make a _____ loop with my rope.
   (run round race)

7. Those _____ cows are mine.
   (when white went)

TRY THIS! Write three sentences about yourself. Use a describing word in each sentence. Then draw a picture to go with your sentences.

Harcourt

SCHOOL-HOME CONNECTION Play the "I Spy" game with your child. One
player uses describing words to tell about something you can both see. The
other player then tries to guess what is being described. Switch roles.

Name _____

▶ **Complete the sentences. Write a Spelling Word from the box on each line.**

where	shall	chin	ship	fish	much

1. "I hurt my _____ when I fell off my horse today."

2. "There is not _____ you can do about it, Jack."

3. "I wish I worked on a _____ out in the ocean."

4. "Don't you remember that you don't like _____?"

5. "I wonder _____ I would be if I worked on a ship."

6. "Let's just think about being cowboys, _____ we?"

Handwriting Tip: When you write the letter *h*, start near the top line.

h

▶ **On each line, write the Spelling Word again.**

7. thank _____   8. white _____

9. each _____   10. thin _____

SCHOOL-HOME CONNECTION Play a spelling game. Write the groups of letters *sh, ch, th,* and *wh* on separate slips of paper. Then turn the slips face down. Take turns choosing a slip and saying a word that begins or ends with those letters. Spell aloud the words you make.

Harcourt

Name _____

▶ **Complete the labels for the pictures of Pam's vacation. Write a word from the box on each line.**

oceans	forcibly	disappoint
stroke	details	information

See the star I found? I didn't know stars

lived in **(1)** _____. I tried

to **(2)** _____ its back.

I wanted to take my star home, but Mom

stopped me **(3)** _____.

"I'm sorry to **(4)** _____ you,
but you have to stay here," I told the star.

"There are a lot of **(5)** _____
about stars in my book, but there isn't any

(6) _____ at all about stars
like you!"

SCHOOL-HOME CONNECTION Ask your child to make a list
of the Vocabulary Words and then to read the words aloud to
you. Talk together about the meaning of each word.

Name _____

▶ **Read the article. Think about the meaning of each underlined word. Then complete the sentences.**

Here Comes Jumbo!

Jumbo is a whale that a whale-watching group spotted in the ocean last week. "We named him Jumbo because he's so <u>immense</u>," said Marty Turner, leader of the group. "We first saw him when he was <u>breaching</u>, or jumping up out of the water."

Jumbo is part of a <u>pod</u>, or group of whales that travel together. He likes to eat tiny sea animals called <u>krill</u>. Jumbo has two big fins called <u>flukes</u> at the end of his tail. He breathes through a kind of nose called a <u>blowhole</u> on the top of his head. Jumbo's thick layer of fat, called <u>blubber</u>, keeps him warm.

1. *Immense* means _____.

2. When a whale jumps out of the water,

   it is called _____.

3. A group of whales that travel

   together is called a _____.

4. *Krill* are _____.

5. The two big fins at the end of a whale's tail are called

   _____.

6. A whale breathes through a _____.

7. *Blubber* is _____.

Harcourt

22 Just in Time

SCHOOL-HOME CONNECTION Write a sentence using a word you think your child may not know. Include a clue to the word's meaning in the sentence. Help your child figure out what the word means.

Name _____

► **Finish the story. On each line, write a word from the box.**

voices	enjoy	toys	join
noise	annoy	choice	point

1. If I had a _____, I would be a whale.

2. I think I would _____ living in the ocean.

3. I would _____ a big family of whales.

4. We would talk with each other in high _____.

5. I would _____ sailors by tossing their boats around.

6. The sailors would _____ at me and say, "Enormous!"

7. I wonder if whales play with balls or

   other _____.

8. I wouldn't make any _____ when the other whales were sleeping.

TRY THIS! Write about what you think it would be like to be a whale. Use as many words as you can that have the same vowel sound as *boy*.

SCHOOL-HOME CONNECTION Ask your child to write a sentence using a word from the box.

Harcourt

Name _____

▶ **Fill in the story map to tell about the story.**

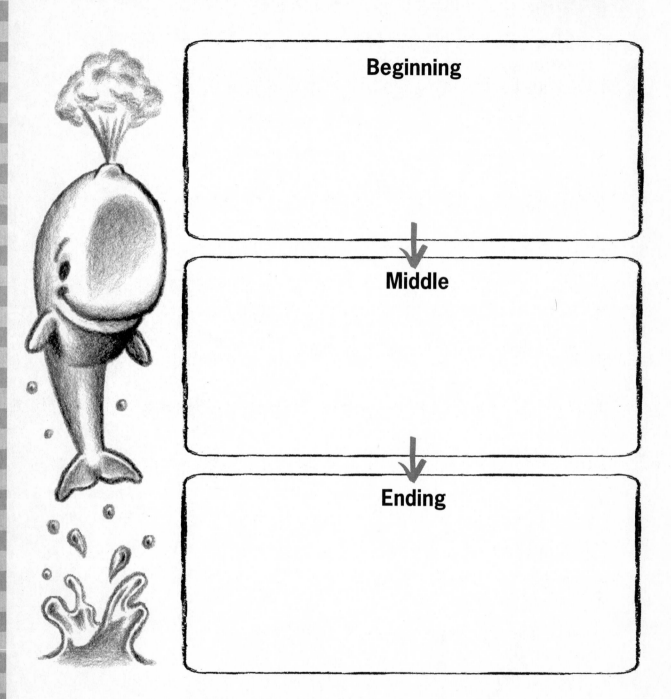

Beginning

Middle

Ending

How do you think Emily feels at the end of the story?

_____

_____

Harcourt

SCHOOL-HOME CONNECTION Ask your child to tell you about Emily's whale in the story "Dear Mr. Blueberry." Ask what Emily learns about whales.

Name _____

▶ **Read the story. Then complete the sentences to tell when each thing happens. Write a word or group of words from the box on each line.**

| today | last night | then | before | at last | tonight | next |

Last night, Hank found a bear in his tub. Before Hank could say anything, the bear started to sing! Then, the bear washed its face and back. Next, it stepped out of the tub and dried its fur on a towel. At last, it walked out of the house. Today, Hank saw the bear rolling in the dirt. Maybe it will have to come back tonight for another bath.

1. Hank found the bear _____.

2. The bear started to sing _____ Hank said anything.

3. The bear _____ washed its face and back.

4. _____, the bear stepped out of the tub.

5. It walked out of the house _____.

6. Hank saw the bear _____.

7. It may even come back _____.

SCHOOL-HOME CONNECTION Ask your child to write three sentences telling what he or she did today. Remind your child to use time words in the sentences.

Harcourt

Name _____

▶ **Read the words under each line. Choose the describing word that tells how something tastes, smells, sounds, or feels. Write it on the line.**

1. Samantha likes _____ snacks.

(saw   sweet   song)

2. Her cat likes _____ snacks.

(salty   say   seed)

3. Samantha eats _____ crackers.

(crunchy   cry   calm)

4. Her cat eats _____ cat food.

(door   dry   do)

5. Samantha likes to listen to her cat's _____ purr.

(loud   let's   lake)

6. She does not like her cat's _____ claws.

(sick   sharp   sorry)

7. Most of all, she likes to rub her cat's _____ fur.

(sat   soft   star)

8. Samantha and her cat _____ together.

(sing   sort   smell)

SCHOOL-HOME CONNECTION Ask your child to tell you about describing words that tell how something tastes, smells, sounds, or feels. Then have your child use describing words in sentences about foods, sounds, and objects he or she likes.

Harcourt

Name _____

It's Probably Good
Dinosaurs Are
Extinct

Vowel Variants:
/ōo/oo, ue,
ew, ui

▶ **Complete the sentences. On each line, write the word that makes sense and has the same vowel sound as *cool, true, chew,* and *suit*.**

1. I sat on the grass and sipped a cup of _____ .
(stoop   juice   milk)

2. I looked up at the _____ sky.
(pink   suit   blue)

3. One cloud was shaped like a _____ .
(boot   bite   boat)

4. Another was long and thin, with curves and _____ .
(pools   loops   lips)

5. I'll give you a _____ about the cloud I saw next.
(clay   clip   clue)

6. It looked like a wise bird that _____ .
(hoots   chirps   hats)

7. It's _____ ! That cloud looked like an owl.
(too   true   tray)

8. Then the wind blew harder, and the owl cloud

_____ away.
(flea   flew   few)

Harcourt

SCHOOL-HOME CONNECTION Ask your child to write the word
fruits on a piece of paper and to draw pictures of different fruits.
Help him or her to label each one.

Name _____

It's Probably Good
Dinosaurs Are
Extinct

Context Clues for
Word Meaning

Social Studies

▶ **Read the article. Think about what each underlined word means. Then answer the questions.**

The State of Alaska

If you're traveling in Alaska, be careful!
<u>Moose</u> walk in the road. These big animals
with huge antlers help make our most
northern state an exciting place. You'll also
find lots of bears and herds of <u>caribou</u>, a kind of reindeer. Alaska has
many <u>glaciers</u>, or large masses of ice, and <u>timber</u>, or trees, near the
coast. Other parts of the country are <u>tundra</u>, which are cold, flat plains
where no trees grow. If you go to Alaska, the <u>chinook</u> may keep you
warm. *Chinook* means the warm, wet wind that blows in
from the sea. You can watch <u>mushers</u>, or dogsled drivers,
race their sleds. You may want to buy a pair of <u>mukluks</u>.
These soft, fur boots will keep your feet warm.

1. What is a moose? _____

2. What is a kind of reindeer found in Alaska? _____

3. What is a glacier? _____

4. What is another word for *trees*? _____

5. What is the tundra like? _____

6. What is the warm wind from the sea called? _____

7. What do mushers drive? _____

8. What are mukluks? _____

SCHOOL-HOME CONNECTION Ask your child to read
this article aloud to you. Talk about how to use clues to
figure out the meaning of an unfamiliar word.

Harcourt

Name _____

▶ **Fill in the web to show the places where dinosaurs would be if they were alive today.**

at the zoo

Places Where
Dinosaurs
Would Be

What is the story mostly about? _____

_____

_____

_____

_____

Harcourt

Name _____

▶ **Read what each person says about a book he or she has read. If the story could happen in real life, write *real-life* on the line. If the story could not happen in real life, write *make-believe* on the line.**

1. I read a book about people who dig up dinosaur bones. They learn what dinosaurs were like. It was a

_____ story.

2. My story was about a mouse that captured a dinosaur

for the zoo. It was a _____ story.

3. I read about a family of ducks that lived on the

moon. That story was _____.

4. My book told about a girl who found a bat in a cave.

It was a _____ story.

5. I read a book about what dinosaurs ate and where

they lived. It was a _____ story.

6. My book was about people riding horses to round up cattle

on the plains. It was a _____ story.

7. I read about a dinosaur that learned to read and

write. It was a _____ story.

8. I read a book about a girl who flew above the city on the tail of a flying dinosaur. This was a

_____ story.

Harcourt

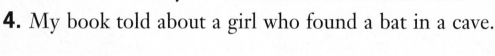 **SCHOOL-HOME CONNECTION** Ask your child to make up a story about a flying cow and to tell the story to you. Then ask him or her to tell which events in the story could happen in real life and which could not.

Name _____

▶ **Read the story events. Decide whether each is
real-life or make-believe. Fill in the circle next
to your choice.**

1 A girl rides a bus across town to visit her grandmother.

⬭ real-life   ⬭ make-believe

2 Two bears go to school, and they learn to read.

⬭ real-life   ⬭ make-believe

3 A boy has a pet dinosaur that helps him do his chores around
the house.

⬭ real-life   ⬭ make-believe

4 A girl finds a bird with a broken wing. She takes it to
the veterinarian.

⬭ real-life   ⬭ make-believe

5 A boy moves to a new town. It's hard for him to make friends.
He joins a club, and soon he has many friends.

⬭ real-life   ⬭ make-believe

6 A girl makes a snowman. When spring comes, the snowman
packs his suitcase and leaves for the North Pole.

⬭ real-life   ⬭ make-believe

Harcourt

Name _____

It's Probably Good
Dinosaurs Are
Extinct

Inflections:
–s, –es,
(change f to v)

▶ **Make each word mean more than one. Write the new word on the line. Follow the examples below.**

　　Examples: *life + s (change f to v) = lives*
　　　　　　　　elf + es (change f to v) = elves

1. loaf + es

_____

2. leaf + es

_____

3. thief + es

_____

4. shelf + es

_____

5. calf + es

_____

6. knife + es

_____

7. wolf + es

_____

8. hoof + es

_____

Harcourt

SCHOOL-HOME CONNECTION Ask your child to write a sentence about a leaf and another sentence about many leaves. Ask him or her to explain to you how the word *leaf* changes to mean more than one.

Name _____

It's Probably Good
Dinosaurs Are
Extinct

Figurative
Language:
Personification

▶ **Read each pair of sentences. On each line,
write a word or group of words that helps tell
what the first sentence means.**

1. A cloud crept in front of the moon.

The cloud moved _____.
(slowly   loudly   quickly)

2. I heard the wind knocking at my door.

The door was _____ in the wind.
(banging   opening   closing)

3. The sun smiled down on the flowers.

The sun _____ the flowers.
(hurt   helped   burned)

4. The rain sang a cheery song at my window.

The sound of the rain was _____.
(spooky   happy   loud)

5. The book called out to Jon to open it.

Jon really _____ to open the book.
(wanted   didn't want   tried)

6. The breeze kissed my nose.

The breeze felt _____ on my nose.
(cold   soft   sharp)

Harcourt

SCHOOL-HOME CONNECTION Ask your child to write
a sentence that uses words to make an object in your
home seem like a person.

Name _____

It's Probably Good
Dinosaurs are
Extinct

**Words That Tell
How Many**

Math

▶ **In each sentence, circle the describing word
that tells how many. Then think of another
describing word that tells how many. Write
your new sentence.**

1. Three boys row on the lake.

_____

2. Two grown-ups help them.

_____

3. They have three fishing poles.

_____

4. They want to catch seven fish.

_____

5. There are five other boats on the lake.

_____

6. Four girls swim in the lake.

_____

7. Ten children fish from the shore.

_____

8. Seven ducks swim by.

_____

SCHOOL-HOME CONNECTION Ask your child to give some
examples of describing words that tell how many. Then take
turns saying funny sentences with these words.

Name _____

▶ **Complete the sentences. Write a Spelling
Word from the box on each line.**

| leaf | leaves | shelf | shelves | elf | elves |

1. I like to draw pictures of _____.

2. Grandma gave me an _____ doll
to put in my room.

3. What a beautiful _____!

4. I will keep it with my other _____.

5. This _____ is getting too full.

6. Dad gave me more _____ for my things.

Handwriting Tip: Do not write letters too close
together or too far apart.

too close	too far apart	just right
lfe	life	life

▶ **On each line, write the Spelling Word again.**

7. wife _____   **8.** wives _____

9. lives _____   **10.** life _____

SCHOOL-HOME CONNECTION With your child, write a story using the
Spelling Words and other words that change the letter *f* to *v* when you
add *-s* or *-es*, such as *wolf/wolves*, *scarf/scarves*, and *knife/knives*.

Just in Time   **39**

Harcourt

Name _____

▶ **Complete the sentences. Write a word from the paint jars on each line.**

mimicked   fussed   pale   admired   notice   haze

Jake liked the **(1)** _____ colors in this painting.

"There's a blue **(2)** _____ over the hills," he said.

In another painting, mother bird **(3)** _____ over

the baby birds. Jake **(4)** _____ the mother bird.

"Did you **(5)** _____ how real that apple looks?"
Jake asked. Can you guess which painting Jake

(6) _____ most of all?

Harcourt

SCHOOL-HOME CONNECTION Play a matching game with your child. Write
each of the Vocabulary Words on two small pieces of paper. Turn the words face
down and mix them up. Take turns with your child turning over two words and
reading them aloud. Play until all the words have been matched.

Name _____

▶ **Read each story beginning. Think about
whether the story is real-life or make-believe.
Then fill in the chart. Complete the sentences, and list
story events.**

Beth's Pictures

Beth loved to paint. She
painted a rainbow on
the barn at Grandpa's
farm. At home, she painted
pictures to hang on her
bedroom wall. At school, she
painted a paper bag to make a
book cover.

1. I know this story is
(real-life   make-believe)

_____

because these things happen.

2. _____

_____

3. _____

_____

4. _____

_____

Cal's Pictures

Cal had a special paintbrush.
He waved his brush in the
air, and there was a
rainbow. He pointed his brush at
the night sky, and stars shone.
When he dipped his brush into
blue paint on a rainy day, the
clouds went away.

5. I know this story is
(real-life   make-believe)

_____

because these things happen.

6. _____

_____

7. _____

_____

8. _____

_____

Harcourt

SCHOOL-HOME CONNECTION Talk with your child about a story he or she has
read. Ask whether the story is real-life or make-believe. Talk with your child about
the story events that show that the story is real-life or that it is make-believe.

Just in Time

Name _____

▶ **Finish the story. On each line, write a word from the box that makes sense.**

roof	chew	cool	fruit
school	blew	true	food

True Winter

I'll tell you a **(1)** _____ story about the storm we had last winter.

At first there was just a

(2) _____ breeze. Then

the wind **(3)** _____ much harder and felt cold. Mom

bought lots of **(4)** _____ at the store in case we had to stay indoors for a week. We had lots of milk and

(5) _____. We even had a bone for our dog

to **(6)** _____. When the storm hit, I was scared

the **(7)** _____ would blow off our house. It snowed so

much that I had to stay home from **(8)** _____ for three days!

Harcourt

SCHOOL-HOME CONNECTION With your child, make up a funny story about a *rooster* that *flew* into a pot of *glue*. Have your child draw a picture of the story and write a caption for it.

Name _____

▶ **Think about the problem in "Cool Ali." Fill in the problem-solution chart.**

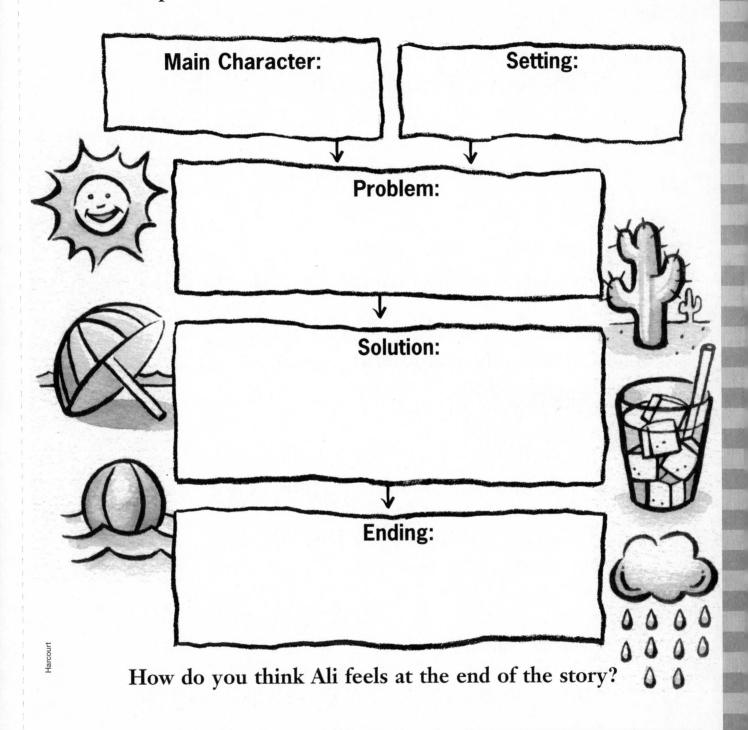

Main Character:

Setting:

Problem:

Solution:

Ending:

How do you think Ali feels at the end of the story?

_____

_____

SCHOOL-HOME CONNECTION Ask your child about the hot day in the
story "Cool Ali." Encourage your child to tell about the pictures Ali draws
and about how her neighbors feel when they see the pictures.

Just in Time **43**

Harcourt

Name _____

▶ **Complete the sentences. On each line, write the word that has the same vowel sound as** *chair* **and that makes sense.**

1. Don't let it _____ you to be up so high! **(skate   score   scare)**

2. Don't drop that _____ of paintbrushes! **(pair   pour   pain)**

3. Don't worry if we _____ at your work. **(store   star   stare)**

4. Do you need more paint from the

    _____ store?
    (hardwood   wore   hardware)

5. Don't let the paint drip into your _____!
    (hair   hurt   her)

6. Take _____ not to fall! **(core   card   care)**

7. Come down the ladder, since you don't have _____.
    (states   starts   stairs)

8. Don't you _____ take a big step back!
    (dart   door   dare)

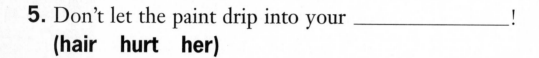

TRY THIS! Use words and pictures to make an ad for something you would like to buy. Use as many words as you can that have the same vowel sound as *chair*.

SCHOOL-HOME CONNECTION Have your child make a list of the words he or she wrote to complete the sentences above. Take turns making up a sentence for each of the words on the list. Say your sentences aloud.

Harcourt

Name _____

▶ **Read the paragraph. On each line, write a word that tells how a character or characters say something.**

Everyone in Mr. Freeman's class was making a flag to hang in the classroom. "We can't wait to start!" chattered Rick and Deb. "Do we really have to be through by noon?" moaned Sammy. "I don't have enough blue paint," Rob complained. "May two of us work together?" whispered Ann. "I spilled the red paint!" cried Don. "Oh, no!" Kay squealed. "Just look at my dress!" Three boys chanted, "Flags are fun. Flags are fun." "I wish everyone would just be quiet," sighed Mr. Freeman.

1. _____   2. _____

3. _____   4. _____

5. _____   6. _____

7. _____   8. _____

TRY THIS! Write about a friend and you talking together. Use words that tell *how* you each say things.

SCHOOL-HOME CONNECTION Ask your child to write a sentence telling something that someone said. Challenge him or her to use a word other than *said* in the sentence.

Harcourt

Name _____

▶ **Finish each sentence. Add *-er* or *-est* to the
describing word in ( ).**

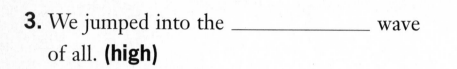

1. The air is _____ than the water. **(warm)**

2. This wave is _____ than that wave. **(high)**

3. We jumped into the _____ wave
   of all. **(high)**

4. My pail is _____ than
   your pail. **(small)**

5. Jake has the _____
   pail of all. **(small)**

6. We can dig the _____ hole on the beach! **(deep)**

7. The water was _____ in the morning than it is
   now. **(cold)**

8. We built the _____ sand castle on the beach. **(tall)**

 TRY THIS! Draw a picture of three short animals that are different sizes.
Write a sentence about each animal. Use the words *short*,
shorter, and *shortest* in your sentences.

Harcourt

SCHOOL-HOME CONNECTION Ask your child to tell you how describing
words are used to compare things. Together, make up sentences that
compare two or more things around your home.

Name _____

▶ **Finish the newspaper story about the art show.**
Write a Spelling Word from the box on each line.

| care | fair | share | scare | pair | rare |

Sara Sims, a second grader at Hilltop

School, won first prize at the state **(1)** _____. Sara painted

a **(2)** _____ of bird pictures. One was an eagle, which is

(3) _____ in this part of the state. "I hope my pictures

make people think about taking better **(4)** _____ of places

where wild birds live," Sara said. "We should not **(5)** _____

them away from their homes." Sara will **(6)** _____ her

pictures with the children at her school.

Handwriting Tip: When you write the letter *r*,
make sure it does not look like the letter *n*.

Harcourt

▶ **On each line, write the Spelling Word again.**

7. dare _____   8. hair _____

9. chair _____   10. air _____

SCHOOL-HOME CONNECTION With your child, make
up a story about someone who shares. In each sentence,
use a word with the sound you hear in *air*.

Just in Time **47**

Name _____

▶ **Complete the sentences. Write a word from the box on each line.**

| mist | still | agreed | gentle | drowsy | lively |

1. Mom _____ to take Ben and me to the park.

2. In the morning we ran and played _____ games.

3. After lunch we were so _____ that we almost went to sleep on the grass.

4. No one moved, and the whole park was very

_____.

5. When a _____ rain began to fall, it was fun to get wet.

6. "We almost missed getting to play in the

_____," Ben joked.

Harcourt

TRY THIS! Draw a picture of you and a friend playing in the rain. Write about your picture. Use as many Vocabulary Words as you can.

SCHOOL-HOME CONNECTION Write each Vocabulary Word on a separate piece of paper. As you hold up each word, ask your child to read it aloud.

Name _____

▶ **Read each story beginning. Then answer the questions.**

Mr. Clark's Lunch Time

It was a warm day. Mr. Clark finished his lunch. He enjoyed sitting on the park bench. The breeze gently brushed his face, and birds sang in the trees.

1. Is "Mr. Clark's Lunch Time" a real-life story or a

make-believe story? _____

2. How can you tell? _____

_____

3. If a dog had jumped up onto the bench and begun to talk with Mr. Clark, would the story be real-life or

make-believe? _____

4. How can you tell? _____

_____

Zippy's Lunch Time

Zippy the Cat loves to play in the park. Today she put on her best cap and her new tennis shoes. Then she hopped on her bike for the short ride to the playground.

5. Is "Zippy's Lunch Time" a real-life story or a make-believe

story? _____

6. How can you tell? _____

_____

SCHOOL-HOME CONNECTION Talk with your child about some of the stories he or she has read in school this year. Ask your child which stories are real-life and which are make-believe, and how he or she can tell.

Just in Time **49**

Harcourt

Name _____

▶ Fill in the web to name some of the people
who visit the park bench and tell what they do there.

Who? old man

What? rests

Who?

What?

People Who Visit
the Park Bench

Who?

What?

Who?

What?

Who?

What?

Who?

What?

SCHOOL-HOME CONNECTION Ask your child to tell you
about the story "The Park Bench." Ask what makes the bench
special and who spends time on it or near it.

Name _____

▶ **Finish the story. On each line, write the word that has the sound at the beginning of *germ* and that makes sense.**

Roger

Roger is a bird who doesn't live in a **(1)** _____.
(tree gate cage) Roger lives in Town Park in a

(2) _____ **(big giant tall)** tree. The tree

is next to the school **(3)** _____.
(gym building yard)

People leave him treats to eat. Once someone even left him a

(4) _____ cookie! **(sugar gingerbread warm)**

Roger lives the best life a bird could **(5)** _____,
(live great imagine) but he is careful. His mother always told

him, "Look out for cats. Cats mean **(6)** _____!
(danger giant help) If you keep out of their way, you will live

to an old **(7)** _____." **(rage gem age)** This is

why Roger never speaks to cats, even the ones that seem to be

(8) _____. **(quiet gentle general)**

TRY THIS! Write a story about a *giraffe* and a park *ranger*. Circle each word in your story that has the sound at the beginning of *giraffe* spelled with the letter *g*.

SCHOOL-HOME CONNECTION Ask your child to write the words *huge* and *gentle* as column headings on a sheet of paper. Then help him or her think of words that name things that are huge or gentle and to write them in the correct column.

Harcourt

Name _____

▶ **Read each sentence and the two meanings that the underlined word may have. Choose the meaning that the word has in the sentence. Write the meaning on the line.**

1. The <u>sign</u> says that this is a one-way street.
(a board that tells what to do, to write one's own name)

_____

2. Let's eat our lunch on the grass in the <u>park</u>.
(an open space where people can play, to stop a car at a place)

_____

3. Don't let the pigs out of the <u>pen</u>!
(a small place with a fence around it, a tool for writing)

_____

4. Our team won the game by one <u>run</u>.
(to move quickly, a point scored in baseball)

_____

5. What <u>kind</u> of cake do you like best? **(nice, sort)**

_____

6. Be sure to give the <u>right</u> answer. **(not left, not wrong)**

_____

7. Grandpa came last week, and he is <u>still</u> here.
(up to this time, quiet)

_____

Harcourt

SCHOOL-HOME CONNECTION Ask your child to write a sentence that has a word with more than one meaning. Your child might like to draw a picture that shows the word's meaning in the sentence.

Name _____

▶ **Complete the sentences. Read the words
under each line. Choose the word that is a verb.
Write it on the line.**

1. I _____ on the bench.
     (so sit stove)

2. You _____ past the bench.
     (walk well way)

3. I _____ hello to you.
     (say she sea)

4. You _____ around.
     (to turn tale)

5. We _____ for a while.
     (talk two table)

6. Then we _____ to the swings.
     (good go green)

7. We _____ there.
     (pill play pond)

8. We _____ home together.
     (walk white whale)

Harcourt

SCHOOL-HOME CONNECTION Ask your child
to tell you what a verb is. Then take turns
acting out different verbs.

Name _____

▶ **Complete the sentences. Write a Spelling Word from the box on each line.**

| bridge | edge | gems | large | change | age |

1. Karen is playing at the _____ of the lake.

2. Her mother is wearing a pin with beautiful _____ .

3. Oh, no! Something has happened to

the _____ sail on Karen's boat.

4. She will _____ boats with her mother.

5. Karen's brothers like to fish from the _____ .

6. They are the same _____ . They are ten years old.

Handwriting Tip: When you write
the letter *g*, make sure it does not
look like the letter *q*.

g   q

▶ **Write a Spelling Word from the box on each line.**

| page | gym | germ | giant |

7. _____

8. _____

9. _____

10. _____

SCHOOL-HOME CONNECTION With your child, use the
Spelling Words to make up rhyming sentences such as
The lights were dim in the gym.

Harcourt

Name _____

▶ **Finish the story. Write a word from the box on each line.**

objects	clasp	cornered
caused	confused	removes	typical

1. May almost never

removes her watch.
One day she left the

clasp open. This
caused her watch
to fall off.

2. Her cat, Sammy, always

spotted _objects_ on
the floor. "This isn't just a

typical cat toy,"
Sammy thought.

3. He picked up the watch.
Then it started to beep!
Sammy was

confused.

4. "Sammy!" May said. "You
have my watch

cornered!"

SCHOOL-HOME CONNECTION Ask your child to read the
Vocabulary Words to you and to tell or show you what each
word means.

Just in Time **55**

Harcourt

Name _____

▶ **Match the words in the box to the clues. Write a word on each line.**

photo	**elephant**	**enough**	**phone**
rough	**dolphin**	**laugh**	**cough**

1. It has a long trunk. _____

2. "Ha, ha!" _____

3. This is a camera picture. _____

4. If you have a cold, you might do this. _____

5. It rings and you answer it. _____

6. See me in the sea! _____

7. If you have plenty, you have this. _____

8. It's not smooth. _____

TRY THIS! Write a funny story about an elephant or a dolphin that takes photos.

 SCHOOL-HOME CONNECTION Have your child write a sentence using two of the words from the box. Ask your child to point out the letters in the words that make the /f/ sound.

Harcourt

Name _____

▶ **Complete the sentences. On each line, write a word from the box that makes sense.**

danger	cages	larger	gems
strange	gentle	regions	imagine

1. Can you _____ talking with a bird?

2. It wouldn't be such a _____ thing to do if you had a pet mynah bird.

3. A mynah bird is a little _____ than a robin.

4. Mynah birds like shiny things like _____.

5. Some mynahs live in the wild, and others are kept

as pets in _____.

6. Many wild mynahs live in _____ where there are farms.

7. They don't seem to be afraid of _____ from humans.

8. Many _____ pet mynahs seem to talk like people do.

TRY THIS! Imagine that you have a pet mynah. Write a story about your bird. Use as many words as you can that have the sound at the beginning of *giant* spelled with the letter *g*.

SCHOOL-HOME CONNECTION Ask your child to imagine a strange animal and to draw a picture of it. Then ask him or her to write about the picture, using the words *imagine* and *strange*.

Harcourt

Name _____

The Pine Park
Mystery

Summarize:
Problem-Solution
Chart

▶ **Think about the problem in "The Pine Park Mystery." Fill in the problem-solution chart.**

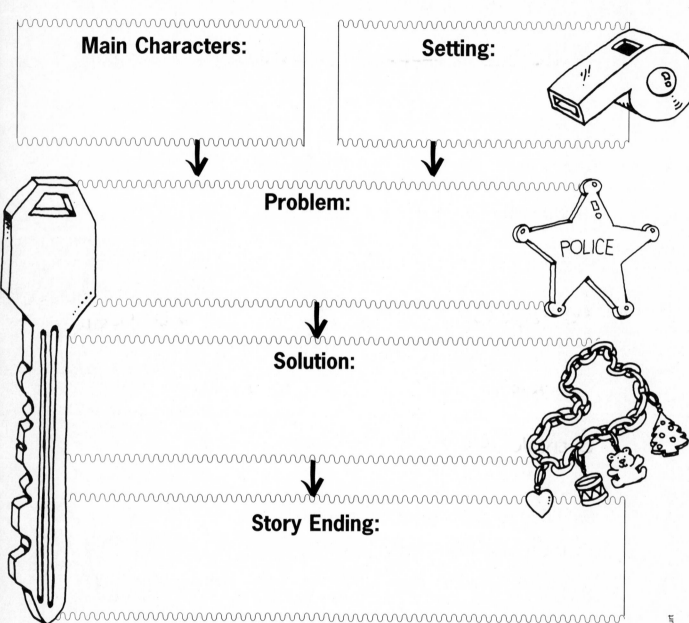

Main Characters:

Setting:

Problem:

Solution:

Story Ending:

What other mysteries do you think Lan and Jeff might discover in the park? _____

Harcourt

SCHOOL-HOME CONNECTION Encourage your child to tell
you about "The Pine Park Mystery." Ask what the mystery is
and how it is solved.

Name _____

▶ **The letters *un* at the beginning of a word mean "not." Add *un* to the beginning of each word in ( ) to complete the sentences. Write the new word on the line.**

Example: un + happy = unhappy (not happy)

1. Mark was _____ how to play his new game. **(sure)**

2. First he _____ all the parts. **(wrapped)**

3. He was still _____ to tell what to do next. **(able)**

4. "The rules of this game are _____!" he cried. **(fair)**

▶ **The letters *re* at the beginning of a word mean "again." Add *re* to the beginning of each word to complete the sentences. Write the new word on the line.**

Example: re + wash = rewash (wash again)

5. Mark _____ the rules of the game. **(read)**

6. "Someone needs to _____ these rules," he said. **(write)**

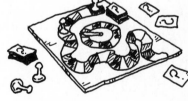

7. "If the rules were _____, this game would be easier to understand." **(done)**

8. "I will try to _____ this game now." **(build)**

Harcourt

SCHOOL-HOME CONNECTION Ask your child to write the word *safe*, and then to add *un* to the beginning of the word. Then talk about things that are safe and unsafe to do.

Name _____

▶ **Read each paragraph. Then answer the questions.**

In every spare moment, Karen played soccer. She took a ball with her everywhere she went. Karen's favorite times were the times she spent with the Blue Sox. Sometimes the girls on the team slept at Karen's house. They made popcorn and talked and talked.

1. How does Karen feel about soccer? _____

_____

2. How can you tell? _____

_____

3. How do you know the girls on Karen's team like her?

_____

Police Chief Polk couldn't solve the mystery of the missing library books. "I know," he said. "I'll call Sal Solvit. He can always figure out a mystery."

Chief Polk called Sal and told him about the problem. "I'll be glad to help," Sal said. "I'll come over just as soon as I finish my homework."

4. What clue tells you that Sal is smart?

_____

Harcourt

SCHOOL-HOME CONNECTION Work with your child to write another paragraph to add to one of the stories on this page. Help your child include story clues that help readers understand an idea that isn't stated in words.

Name _____

▶ **Solve the riddles. Write a word or group of words from the box on each line.**

mayor	coach	teacher	bookstore owner
baker	doctor	writer	farmer

1. This person shows others how to play a sport. Who is it?

a _____

2. If you grow plants on lots of land, who are you?

a _____

3. This person sells books. Who is it?

a _____

4. This person helps children learn to read. Who is it?

a _____

5. If you make bread and cakes in your shop, who are you?

a _____

6. This person is the head of a city. Who is it?

a _____

7. If you make up stories and put them on paper, who are you?

a _____

8. This person helps people who are sick. Who is it?

a _____

Harcourt

SCHOOL-HOME CONNECTION Talk with your child about various careers he or she might have one day. Help your child make a list of possible careers.

Name _____

▶ **Finish each sentence. Write the verb that is in
( ). Add the letter *s* if it is needed.**

1. The birds _____ up twigs. **(pick)**

2. They _____ them to their nest. **(add)**

3. One bird _____ food. **(bring)**

4. The other bird _____ in
the nest. **(wait)**

5. We _____ at the nest every day. **(look)**

6. One day we _____ baby birds. **(hear)**

7. Tad _____ the little birds first. **(see)**

8. My friends and I _____ birds! **(like)**

**TRY
THIS!** With a partner, choose an animal. Take turns saying
sentences about what one animal does and what many
animals do. Be sure to add *s* to the verb when your
sentence tells about just one animal.

Harcourt

SCHOOL-HOME CONNECTION Ask your child when the letter *s* is added to the
end of a verb. Have your child write a sentence that tells what one friend does.
Then help your child change the sentence to tell what many friends do.

Name _____

The Pine Park
Mystery
**Words That End
with -s, -ed,
and -ing**

▶ **Complete the sentences. Write a Spelling
Word from the box on each line.**

playing	helped	eats
blowing	looking	turned

1. My baby bird ____turned____ into a big bird.

2. My bird ____eats____ from my hand.

3. When the wind is ____blowing____ my bird
likes to be inside.

4. I spend lots of time ____playing____ with
my bird.

5. I am _____ for another bird.

6. I _____ my bird when it broke its wing.

Handwriting Tip: When you write the
letter *s*, make sure it faces the correct way,
like this:

____S____

▶ **On each line, write the Spelling Word again.**

7. missing _____   **8. singing** _____

9. stops _____   **10. kids** _____

SCHOOL-HOME CONNECTION Make flash cards using the following
words: *bark, end, help, open,* and *paint.* Have your child choose a card.
Then ask your child to add *-s, -ed,* or *-ing* to the word and to spell it.

Name _____

▶ **Complete the sentences. Write a word from the box on each line.**

| route | pour | honor | clerk | grown | addresses |

We Love You, Mrs. King!

We are having a party in _____ of Mrs. King.

She drives the bus on our _____ .

My brother is _____ up now, but he used to ride Mrs. King's bus, too.

She must know the _____ of hundreds of students!

I'll go to the store and ask the _____ to order us a cake.

I'll _____ cold drinks for everybody.

SCHOOL-HOME CONNECTION With your child, make up a story using the Vocabulary Words. Then have your child draw a picture for the story.

Harcourt

Name _____

▶ **Read each story beginning. Then answer the questions. Write your answers on the lines.**

Mr. Bruce thought he had the perfect job. He liked walking around the town. He liked bringing letters and cards to people who had been waiting for them. Most of all he liked seeing all the friendly people that lived in the houses that he passed every day.

1. Mr. Bruce's job is _____

2. How do you know? _____

_____

_____

Duke was one of Mr. Bruce's best friends. Every day when Mr. Bruce came up the street, Duke ran to meet him. Duke's tail wagged and he barked happily as Mr. Bruce gave him a treat.

3. What kind of animal is Duke? _____

4. How do you know? _____

_____

Harcourt

► **Fill in the story map to tell what happens in the beginning, middle, and ending of "Good-bye, Curtis."**

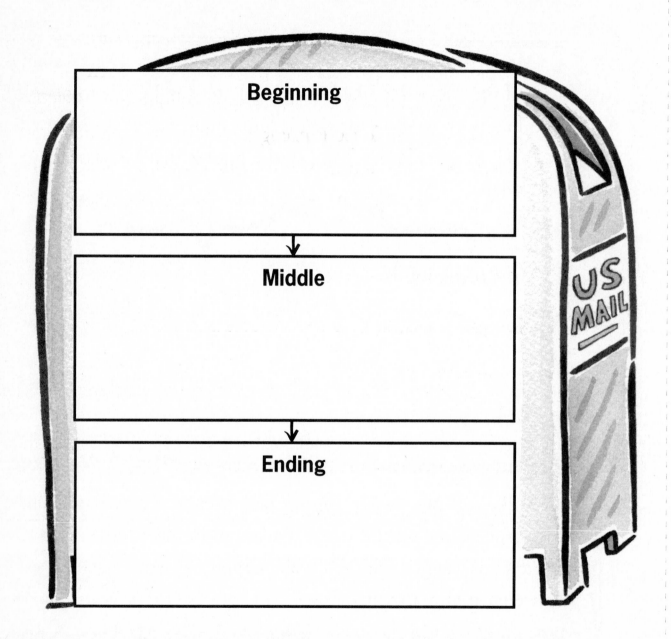

Beginning

Middle

Ending

What is the story mostly about?

_____

_____

SCHOOL-HOME CONNECTION Ask your child to tell you about the story "Good-bye, Curtis." Ask how the people on Curtis's mail route surprise him.

Harcourt

Name _____

▶ **Read the paragraph. Then complete the sentences.**

Last week Mr. Lester went back to the town where he grew up. It had been many years since he had been there. He found many surprises. The old school was gone. Mr. Lester had loved learning to read in that school. Mr. Lester found the house where he had lived. It looked almost the same as it had when he was young. The same trees were in the back yard.

Important Events

1. Mr. Lester went _____.

2. He found many _____.

Less Important Events

3. Mr. Lester had not been to the town in _____.

4. At school Mr. Lester had loved _____.

5. Behind Mr. Lester's old house were _____.

· ·

6. This paragraph is mostly about _____

_____.

TRY THIS! Think of another story you have read. Write a sentence that tells what the story is mostly about.

SCHOOL-HOME CONNECTION Ask your child to tell you about one of the stories he or she has read at school. Then ask him or her to make a list of the most important events in the story and to write a sentence about each one.

Just in Time **67**

Harcourt

Name _____

▶ **Read the paragraph. Choose the best answer to each question. Fill in the circle next to your choice.**

It was a hot day, and Mollie and Glenn were working hard. They were helping get ready for a party to welcome a new family to the neighborhood. There was so much to do! Officer Foster would keep cars from parking on their street while the party was going on. Without cars, they could play games in the street safely. Glenn wanted to play kickball. Mollie and Glenn helped set up the chairs that the grown-ups brought. They helped with the food, too. There would be hot dogs, chips, and watermelon. Mollie loved watermelon!

1 Which of these events is important enough to be put in a summary of the paragraph?
- ⬭ Mollie loved watermelon.
- ⬭ The grown-ups brought chairs.
- ⬭ Mollie and Glenn helped with the food and chairs.

2 Which of these events is not important enough to be in the summary?
- ⬭ Mollie and Glenn helped get ready for the party.
- ⬭ The party was a way to welcome a new family.
- ⬭ It was a hot day.

3 Which of these events should also be put in the summary?
- ⬭ Mollie and Glenn worked hard for the party.
- ⬭ The day was hot.
- ⬭ There would be chips to go with the hot dogs.

4 Which of these sentences tells what the paragraph is mostly about?
- ⬭ It was a hot day.
- ⬭ Mollie and Glenn helped get ready for a party for a new family.
- ⬭ Officer Foster kept cars off the street.

Harcourt

Name _____

▶ **Complete the sentences. Write a compound word on each line, by putting together a word from box 1 with a word from box 2.**

box 1 | after   grand   back   thank-   mail   good-   side   hand

box 2 | yard   walk   bye   children   you   box   shake   shave

1. Last week, I found a letter in my _____.

2. It was an invitation to a party in Mr. Baker's

_____.

3. I bought a bottle of _____ to give
to Mr. Baker.

4. On the day of the party, there was a sign near

Mr. Baker's _____.

5. Everyone gave Mr. Baker a _____
or a big hug.

6. I had fun playing tag with Mr. Baker's

two _____.

7. When I left, I said _____ to Mr. Baker
and thanked him for inviting me.

8. Today I got a _____ note from
Mr. Baker!

SCHOOL-HOME CONNECTION Ask your child to draw a picture that
shows what the weather is like today. Then help him or her write a compound word about the weather, such as *rainstorm*, *overcast*, or *sunshine*.

Harcourt

Name _____

▶ **Finish each sentence. Change the verb in ( ) to tell about the past. Write it on the line.**

1. Yesterday, Mrs. Yee _____ up to our door. **(walk)**

2. She _____ the doorbell. **(push)**

3. Dad _____ the door. **(open)**

4. Mrs. Yee _____ Dad with a big box. **(greet)**

5. Dad _____ Mrs. Yee. **(thank)**

6. Then Dad _____ the box to me. **(pass)**

7. I _____, "Is it really for me?" **(ask)**

8. Dad _____ to my name on the box. **(point)**

TRY THIS! Write four sentences about something you did last week. In your sentences, use verbs that end with *-ed*. Then draw a picture to go with your sentences.

SCHOOL-HOME CONNECTION Ask your child to explain when to use verbs that end with *-ed*. Together, talk about what your family did yesterday. Point out the verbs that end with *-ed*.

Harcourt

Name _____

▶ **Match the Spelling Words to the picture clues. Write a Spelling Word on each line.**

mailbox	cupcake	cannot
inside	classroom	myself

 1. _____

 2. _____

 3. _____

 4. _____

 5. _____

 6. _____

Handwriting Tip: When you write the letter *b*, make a circle that touches the stem.

▶ **On each line, write the Spelling Word again.**

7. bathtub _____   8. bedroom _____

9. backyard _____   10. birthday _____

Harcourt

SCHOOL-HOME CONNECTION Play a matching game with your child. On separate cards, write individual words that can combine to make compound words, such as *in*, *out*, *side*, and *doors*. Turn the cards face down. Take turns trying to make a match.

Name _____

▶ **Finish the story. Write a word from the drums
on each line.**

rhythm

conductor

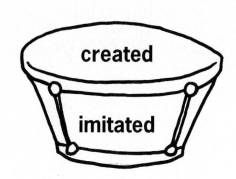

created

imitated

appeared

startled

Jen asked Mr. Strong, the train **(1)** _____, for

an old box. She put a lid on the box and **(2)** _____

a drum. Slowly she began to beat out a **(3)** _____ .

Boom boom–boom BOOM! The noise **(4)** _____ two
girls who were walking by. "I like that sound. Let's dance!" one of
them said.

Then a man and a woman **(5)** _____ . They

both **(6)** _____ the steps the girls were doing. Soon
all the people on the street had gathered to tap their feet!

SCHOOL-HOME CONNECTION Write each Vocabulary Word on a
separate piece of paper. Hide the words around your home. Challenge
your child to find all the words and read them aloud to you.

Harcourt

Name _____

▶ **Label the pictures. Write a word from the box on each line.**

giraffe	**pigeon**	**ranger**	**gerbil**
page	**cage**	**garbage**	**engine**

(1) _____

(2) _____

(3) _____ in a (4) _____

fire (5) _____

(6) _____

(7) _____ can

park (8) _____

TRY THIS! Write a story to tell why the giraffe is walking through the park. Use as many words as you can that have the sound at the beginning of *giant* spelled with the letter *g*.

SCHOOL-HOME CONNECTION Ask your child to write a story about what it would be like to be a pigeon in a park. Ask him or her to point out the words that have the sound at the beginning of *giant* spelled with the letter *g*.

Harcourt

▶ **Complete the sentences. Use the letters *un* or *re* to make a new word that means the same as the two words in ( ). Write the new word on the line.**

1. Amber had never marched in a parade

before, and she was _____
just what to do. **(not sure)**

2. "What if I'm _____ to play my drum and march at the same time?" she wondered. **(not able)**

3. Just then her friend Sherry _____
at her side. **(appeared again)**

4. "Don't be _____," Sherry said. **(not happy)**

5. "If you're _____ about what to do, just follow the person in front of you." **(not clear)**

6. "You'll _____ the same rhythm over and over as you march," said Sherry. **(play again)**

7. Soon Amber was marching and drumming the

_____ rhythm perfectly. **(not changing)**

8. When she _____ Sherry after the parade, she was smiling happily. **(joined again)**

Harcourt

SCHOOL-HOME CONNECTION Ask your child to write sentences using the words *unlock* and *retell*. Ask him or her to tell you what the prefixes *un-* and *re-* mean.

Name _____

▶ **Read the newspaper story and the sentences.
Write *yes* after each sentence that belongs in a summary of
the story. Write *no* after each sentence that does not belong
in a summary of the story.**

Talent Show at Youth Center

Children from Elm Grove put on a show
Saturday night at the Youth Center. Groups
of children sang and danced on the stage.
Decorations were made by the second-grade
class at Smith School. Mr. John W. Hill was
in charge of the show. The children made
many kinds of music and dressed in colorful
costumes. The show raised more than $200 for
the town library.

1. Children from Elm Grove gave a talent show. _____

2. Mr. Hill was in charge of the show. _____

3. Students made their own costumes. _____

4. The second-grade class made decorations. _____

5. The show was good. _____

6. The talent show raised money for the town library. _____

SCHOOL-HOME CONNECTION Tell your child a story
about something that happened this week. Then ask him or
her to write a summary of the story.

Harcourt

Name _____

▶ **Finish the story. On each line, write a word from the box.**

dare	pair	stairs	share
care	scared	hair	air

Off to the State Fair

"Susan!" called Mother from the top of the

(1) _____. "It's time go!" Susan brushed

her **(2)** _____ and put on her new **(3)** _____

of shoes. Then she ran through the cool morning

(4) _____ to the family car. "You can

(5) _____ the back seat with Tick Tock," Mother said.

"Don't be **(6)**_____, Tick Tock," Susan said to her pet

rooster. "I'll take good **(7)** _____ of you. You may

even win a prize today. I **(8)** _____ anyone to have a

more beautiful rooster!"

 TRY THIS! Write what you think will happen to Susan and Tick Tock at the fair. Use some words from the box.

SCHOOL-HOME CONNECTION Ask your child to pick two words from the box. Then have your child use the words in two sentences. Have your child draw a picture to go with his or her sentences.

Harcourt

Name _____

▶ **Fill in the flowchart to show the order of events in the story.**

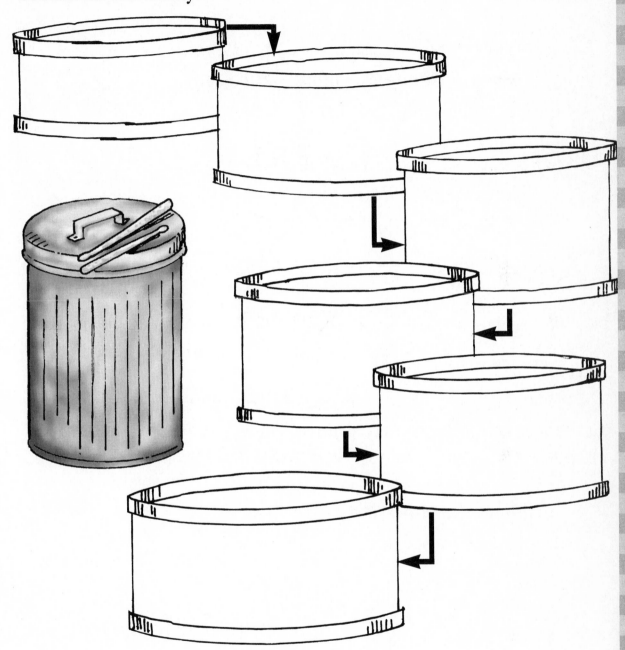

What do you think Max will do with his real drumsticks?

_____

_____

SCHOOL-HOME CONNECTION Encourage your child to tell you about Max in the story "Max Found Two Sticks." Ask what exciting thing happens to Max at the end of the story.

Name _____

▶ **Finish the story. On each line, write the word
that has the same vowel sound as *you* and that makes sense.**

Scott ran **(1)** _____

(thought   think   through)

the house shouting, "Mom!

(2) _____ will never guess

(You   Your   Yourself)

what I'm going to do! There's a talent

show at the **(3)** _____

(Town   Park   Youth)

Center next week. **(4)** _____

(Lon   Lane   Lou)

and I are going to play drums. There will be a

(5) _____ of folk dancers, and we will

(grip   group   trio)

drum while they dance."

Mom smiled. "I just knew **(6)** _____ get to

(yard   year   you'd)

play those drums in a show some day."

 TRY THIS! Write about a show you have seen or imagined. Use at
least one word that has the vowel sound in *you* spelled
ou or *ough*.

 SCHOOL-HOME CONNECTION Have your child make a list of the
words he or she wrote to complete the sentences. Take turns making up
a sentence for each of the words on the list. Say your sentences aloud.

Harcourt

Name _____

▶ **Complete the sentences. Write a sound word from the box on each line.**

| cluck crash clatter tap dingdong thud crunch growl |

1. The dry leaves _____ under my feet in the autumn.

2. I dropped the big book, and it fell to the floor

with a dull _____ .

3. The _____ of pots and pans told me that Dad was cooking dinner.

4. We heard the raindrops _____ softly on our window.

5. The hen will _____ when she lays an egg.

6. The doorbell rang its loud _____ .

7. The bear's _____ told us it was angry.

8. Look out! The ball is going to _____ through the window!

TRY THIS! Make a list of sound words that tell what you hear when you play your favorite outdoor game. Write a sentence using one of the words.

SCHOOL-HOME CONNECTION Help your child write a story about a day in the city or in the country. Use as many sound words as you can.

Harcourt

Name _____

▶ **These sentences tell about now. Write *am*, *is*,**
   or *are* to complete each sentence.

1. This drum _____ big.

2. It _____ a gift for me.

3. I _____ very happy!

4. My dogs _____ happy, too.

▶ **These sentences tell about the past.**
   Write *was* or *were* to complete
   each sentence.

5. Mr. Fox _____ my drum teacher.

6. Tasha and Sophie _____ in the
   class, too.

7. We _____ good drummers.

8. I _____ the best!

 TRY THIS! Work with a partner. Take turns telling about yourselves.
Use the verbs *am*, *is*, *was*, and *were*.

Harcourt

SCHOOL-HOME CONNECTION Ask your child to say
sentences using the verbs *am*, *is*, and *are*. Then ask your child
to change those sentences to use the verbs *was* and *were*.

Name _____

▶ **Finish the story. Write a Spelling Word from the box on each line.**

| throughway | cougar | group | youth | soup | through |

1. A day of fun was planned for the _____ of the town.

2. First, they saw a _____ at the zoo.

3. Then, they rode a bus on the _____.

4. For lunch, the _____ stopped at a park.

5. They ate sandwiches and _____.

6. Then, everyone ran _____ the park.

Handwriting Tip: When you write the letter *o*, make sure you make a full circle.

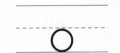

▶ **Write a Spelling Word from the box on each line.**

| throughout | coupon | you | wound |

7. _____   8. _____

9. _____   10. _____

SCHOOL-HOME CONNECTION With your child, make up three sentences, using as many Spelling Words as you can.

Harcourt

Name _____

▶ **Finish the ad. Write a word from the box on each line.**

landscape business dappled exhibition thousands ranch

Come and stay for a week or two at Misty Meadow!

MISTY MEADOW

Y ou will love your vacation at our

beautiful _____. You may want to ride a

_____ horse across the hills. Make a lasso and take

part in a roping _____. Walk in our new flower

garden, cared for by our own _____.

At Misty Meadow, you will feel you are _____
of miles from the city!

TRY THIS! Draw a picture of a place where you would like to go on vacation. Write two or three sentences about your picture. Use as many vocabulary words as you can.

SCHOOL-HOME CONNECTION Ask your child to draw a picture of a ranch and to label the picture, using as many Vocabulary Words as possible.

Harcourt

Name _____

▶ **Read each paragraph. The main idea is underlined. Write four details from the paragraph that support the main idea.**

Arizona is a very dry state. Its name even means "dry land." Some of its rivers run only part of the year. Since it rains so little, farmers have to bring water to their fields through ditches and pipes. Much of the south and west part of the state is desert.

1. _____

2. _____

3. _____

_____

4. _____

Even though it is dry, Arizona has some beautiful places. The Grand Canyon is exciting to see. Rocks in odd shapes glow red and yellow against the bright blue sky. Arizona also has some thick, green forests. There is even an amazing forest where the logs have turned to stone!

5. _____

6. _____

_____

7. _____

8. _____

_____

SCHOOL-HOME CONNECTION Ask your child to read the paragraphs on this page aloud to you. Then ask him or her to point out the supporting details in each paragraph.

Harcourt

▶ **Read the paragraphs. Then read the summary sentences at the bottom of the page. Match each sentence to the paragraph it summarizes and write it on the lines.**

Will Rogers was one of America's famous cowboys. He was born in Oklahoma and was part Native American. Will was an expert at riding and roping, but he was known best for the funny stories he wrote and told.

1. _____

_____

Another famous cowboy was Roy Rogers. Roy Rogers wasn't a real cowboy, but he played one in movies. He also sang cowboy songs and had his own TV show. Many of his films and shows were made with his wife, Dale Evans.

2. _____

_____

Summary Sentences

Roy Rogers was a movie cowboy who sang cowboy songs and had his own TV show.

Will Rogers was a famous American cowboy who was known for riding, roping, and telling funny stories.

Harcourt

SCHOOL-HOME CONNECTION Tell your child a story about something that happened when you were a child. Then ask him or her to write a short summary of the story.

Name _____

▶ **Solve the riddles. Add *un* or *re* to a word in the
box to make a new word. Write the new word on each line.**

button	write	lock
wash	wrap	read
buckle	fill	

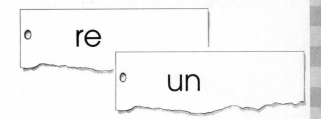

1. What do you do when someone gives you a present?

You _____ it.

2. What do you do when you need to open a door?

You _____ it.

3. What do you do when your glass of milk is empty?

You _____ it.

4. What do you do when you don't understand a paragraph?

You _____ it.

5. What do you do before you take off your coat?

You _____ it.

6. What do you do when something you washed isn't clean?

You _____ it.

7. What do you do before you get out of a car?

You _____ your seat belt.

8. What do you do when you don't like a story you wrote?

You _____ it.

Harcourt

SCHOOL-HOME CONNECTION Ask your child to draw a
picture of something that can be reused over and over and to
label the picture.

▶ **Think about what you learned from "Anthony Reynoso: Born to Rope." Fill in the web with six facts about Anthony.**

What kinds of things do you think Anthony will teach his younger brother or sister?

_____

_____

SCHOOL-HOME CONNECTION Ask your child to tell you about Anthony in the story "Anthony Reynoso: Born to Rope." Ask what roping tricks Anthony Reynoso could do.

Harcourt

Name _____

▶ **Read the paragraphs. Then answer the
questions. Write your answers on the lines.**

Every year there is a roping contest in our town. Some
people dance inside a spinning rope. Some people hold the rope
between their teeth! The best ropers win prizes.

What sentence tells the main idea?

1. _____

What three sentences tell important details?

2. _____

3. _____

4. _____

The water park has something for everyone. My sister jumps
off the diving board. My younger brother swims where the water
isn't deep. My mom likes to sit in the shade.

What sentence tells the main idea?

5. _____

What three sentences tell important details?

6. _____

7. _____

8. _____

Harcourt

SCHOOL-HOME CONNECTION Ask your child to write a
paragraph about something he or she likes to do with a friend.
Then ask your child to point out the main idea of the paragraph.

▶ **Read the paragraphs. Choose the best answer to each question. Fill in the circle next to your choice.**

There is a lot of work to do at Grandma's restaurant. Of course, someone has to cook the food. Someone else greets people at the door. Sometimes my grandmother carries the food to the tables. Then other people clean off the tables and wash the dishes.

1 Which sentence tells the main idea?

- ○ Grandma sometimes carries the food.
- ○ Others clean off the tables and wash dishes.
- ○ There is a lot of work to do at Grandma's restaurant.

2 Which sentence tells an important detail?

- ○ Working at a restaurant is hard.
- ○ Someone must cook the food.
- ○ People want to eat.

Slim is a cowhand who always has his hat. Slim's hat keeps the sun out of his eyes on sunny days, and it keeps his head dry on rainy days. He waves his hat to make the cows move the way they should. Sometimes he fills his hat with water to give his horse a drink. A cowhand's hat is used in many different ways.

3 Which sentence tells the main idea?

- ○ Slim's hat keeps the sun out of his eyes.
- ○ Sometimes he fills his hat with water.
- ○ A cowhand's hat is used in many different ways.

4 Which sentence tells an important detail?

- ○ It's sunny on the ranch.
- ○ Every cowhand should have a hat.
- ○ Slim rides a horse.
- ○ Slim's hat keeps his head dry on rainy days.

Harcourt

Name _____

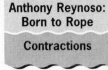

▶ **Read the story. On each line, write the two words that make up the underlined contraction.**

(1) I'm glad I live on a ranch. Every day **(2)** there's something new to do. In the mornings I **(3)** can't wait to get on my horse and ride across the hills. Even when **(4)** it's raining, I love to ride. Sometimes in the afternoon, when **(5)** everything's quiet, I help Dad feed the cows. Dad **(6)** wouldn't like to have to do all the work alone. He says **(7)** we're a good team here on the ranch. I know **(8)** that's right!

1. _____

2. _____

3. _____

4. _____

5. _____

6. _____

7. _____

8. _____

Just in Time **89**

▶ **Complete the sentences. Write *has*, *have*, or *had* on each line.**

1. Meg _____ an old rope last year.

2. Now she _____ a new rope.

3. Her brothers _____ ropes now, too.

4. They _____ many hours of practice last week.

5. Yesterday, they _____ a show.

6. Now they _____ fun with their ropes.

7. The horses _____ fun now, too.

8. Now Meg _____ a prize!

TRY THIS! Play a drawing game with a partner. Take turns drawing part of a picture. When you finish your part, tell your partner what the picture had before and what it has now. Go on drawing and talking until your picture is done.

Harcourt

SCHOOL-HOME CONNECTION Ask your child to tell you what he or she has learned about using *has*, *have*, and *had* in sentences. Then ask your child to say three sentences that use those three words.

Name _____

▶ **The Spelling Words are contractions of the underlined words in the sentences. On each line, write the contraction that is made by the underlined words.**

don't	I've	we're	I'll	can't	you're

I have got a big hat.

1. _____

Joey, you are my friend.

2. _____

Jeffrey, we are going to have fun.

3. _____

I will be right in!

4. _____

Please do not let the dog in!

5. _____

I can not stop him.

6. _____

Handwriting Tip: When you write, make sure you leave enough space between the letters.

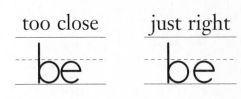

too close   just right

be   be

▶ **On each line, write the Spelling Word again.**

7. you'll _____

8. they've _____

9. they'll _____

10. we'll _____

SCHOOL-HOME CONNECTION With your child, make up three sentences, using several of the Spelling Words. Have your child write the sentences.

Just in Time **91**

Harcourt

▶ **Complete the sentences. Write a word from the box on each line.**

looming	fleet	horizon	cozy
realized	launched		drifted

1. On Saturday morning, Will _____ his new boat.

2. "It's not part of a _____, but it will get there just fine on its own."

3. All day Will's boat _____ slowly along.

4. Once he had to turn the boat almost sideways when he saw

a big rock _____ in front of him.

5. As the sun set over the _____, Will squinted at his watch.

6. He _____ he must head for home.

7. "Boats are nice, but at night a _____ house is best," he said.

SCHOOL-HOME CONNECTION Write each Vocabulary Word on a separate piece of paper. Then cut each word apart to make puzzles. Help your child put the words together and read them aloud.

Harcourt

Name _____

▶ **Read the paragraphs. On each line, write the sentence from the paragraph that tells what the paragraph is mostly about.**

The mole's front paws have long nails. It uses its front legs like shovels to scoop out dirt as it digs for food. Its back legs are short and strong. A mole is good at digging.

1. _____

Many moles live most of their lives underground. Sometimes you can find a mole's house by looking for the mound of dirt above it. Moles make nests about a foot under the ground and line them with leaves. They even look for food, such as worms and insects, underground.

2. _____

One kind of mole makes an underground house with many rooms. The rooms are connected by tunnels. One tunnel is an exit that the mole can use in case of danger. The mole makes its nest in the room in the middle.

3. _____

_____

TRY THIS! Imagine you are a mole. Write a paragraph about what it would be like to live in an underground house. Underline the main idea of your paragraph.

SCHOOL-HOME CONNECTION Ask your child to read a paragraph on this page aloud to you and to tell how he or she found the main idea.

Just in Time **93**

Harcourt

Name _____

▶ **Finish the story. On each line, write a word
from the box.**

| youthful | through | you | toucan | Lou | soup |

1. Have _____ met Big Bill?

2. He's a _____ .

3. Big Bill loves to eat noodle _____ .

4. He shares it with his

friend _____ .

5. Bill sips milkshakes _____ a straw.

6. He says that milkshakes keep his feathers

looking _____ .

 **TRY
THIS!** Draw a funny picture of a bird. Write a sentence about your
picture. Use one of the words from the box in your sentence.

SCHOOL-HOME CONNECTION With your child, make up
another story about Big Bill the Toucan. Ask your child to
write a sentence about the story, using the word *toucan*.

Harcourt

Name _____

▶ **Fill in the story map to tell what happens in the beginning, middle, and ending of "Montigue on the High Seas."**

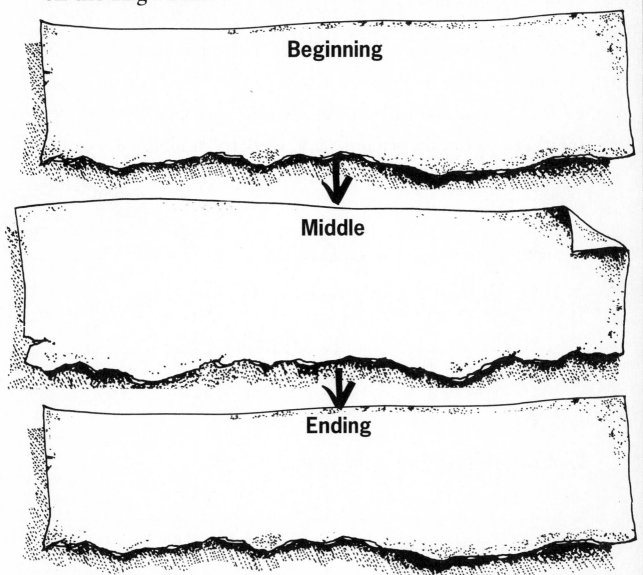

Beginning

Middle

Ending

Harcourt

Which part of this story do you like best? _____

_____

_____

SCHOOL-HOME CONNECTION Ask your child to tell you about the story "Montigue on the High Seas." Ask what kind of animal Montigue is and how he and the mice escape from the ship.

Name _____

▶ **Read the story. Then answer the questions
about the causes and the effects of the story events.
Write a sentence on each line.**

Milo the mouse wished he could fly. Betty the bird wanted to
help, so she let Milo hop onto her back. Flying through the sky
made Milo feel sick, so he shut his eyes. He couldn't see
anything! Drops of rain began to fall, so Betty landed
under a park bench. Milo felt better on the
ground. He knew he wouldn't
want to fly again.

1. Why did Betty let Milo hop onto her back?

_____

2. Why did Milo shut his eyes?

_____

3. What happened when Milo shut his eyes?

_____

4. What happened when the rain started to fall?

_____

TRY THIS! What would you do if it started to rain when you were
outside? Write a sentence that tells a cause and an effect.

Harcourt

SCHOOL-HOME CONNECTION Tell your child about
something exciting that has happened to you. Ask your
child to write the cause and the effect.

Name _____

▶ **Read the sentences. Choose the best answer to each question. Fill in the circle next to your choice.**

1 The wind blew so hard that the sailboat tipped over. Why did the sailboat tip over?

- ⬯ The wind blew hard.
- ⬯ The boat was a sailboat.
- ⬯ The boat was on the sea.

2 The tall waves spilled over the boat, and everyone got wet. What happened because the waves spilled over the boat?

- ⬯ The waves spilled over the boat.
- ⬯ The waves were tall.
- ⬯ Everyone got wet.

3 Two men made a big fire on the beach, so the people got warm. How did the people get warm?

- ⬯ Two men made a fire.
- ⬯ The fire was on the beach.
- ⬯ The fire was big.

4 The little boat sank, so everyone swam to shore. Why did everyone swim to shore?

- ⬯ The waves were tall.
- ⬯ The boat sank.
- ⬯ The shore was nearby.

5 The pilot of a plane found the people because she saw the fire. What happened because of the fire?

- ⬯ The pilot was flying in a plane.
- ⬯ The pilot found the people.
- ⬯ The pilot was a woman.

6 The pilot sent help, so all the people got home safely. What happened because the pilot sent help?

- ⬯ The people began to eat.
- ⬯ No one asked for help.
- ⬯ All the people got home safely.

Harcourt

Name _____

Montigue on the
High Seas

Figurative
Language with
Multiple-Meaning
Words

▶ **Read each numbered sentence. Think about
the underlined words. Then choose the answer
that tells what the numbered sentence really
means. Write your choice on the line.**

1. Mouse wanted to sail <u>the high seas</u>.

Mouse wanted to feel taller in the ocean.

Mouse wanted to sail far out in the ocean.

_____

2. One day his little boat was <u>swept out to sea</u>.

The sailors on the boat cleaned it with a broom.

The water took the boat into the ocean quickly.

_____

3. Raindrops <u>as hard as nails</u> thumped Mouse's head.

It wasn't easy for Mouse to feel the raindrops.

The raindrops hurt Mouse's head.

_____

4. "Hold on for <u>a rocky ride</u>!" said a fish.

The ride will not be smooth.

There will be rocks in the ocean.

_____

SCHOOL-HOME CONNECTION Ask your child to find words
on this page that have more than one meaning, such as *swept*,
and to draw pictures to illustrate their meanings.

Harcourt

Name _____

▶ **Read the words under each line. Write the correct form of the verb to finish the sentence.**

1. Years ago, Ms. Burk _____ a boat that she liked.
(see saw)

2. She _____ a man money and bought it.
(gave gives)

3. Now she _____ the boat every day.
(see sees)

4. Other people _____ the boat, too.
(see sees)

5. The people _____ Ms. Burk some money.
(gives give)

6. She _____ them a ride on the boat.
(gives give)

7. Last week, the people on the boat _____ a whale.
(sees saw)

8. The whale _____ everyone a thrill.
(give gave)

TRY THIS! With a partner, talk about things you see now and things you saw last summer. Use the words *see*, *sees*, and *saw*.

SCHOOL-HOME CONNECTION Ask your child to tell you how the verb *give* changes when it tells about the past. Then ask your child about gifts he or she has received. Encourage your child to use the verbs *give*, *gives*, and *gave* in answering.

Harcourt

Name _____

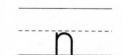

▶ **Finish the letter. Write a Spelling Word from the box on each line.**

| loved | having | saved | lived | hoped | coming |

Dear Grandma,

Thank you for the book. I **(1)** _____

the story about how the mice **(2)** _____
the day. I liked reading about how they

(3) _____ together and were happy. I **(4)** _____
they would get away from the cat, and they did!

I am **(5)** _____ fun with my friends. Are you

(6) _____ to visit soon?
Love,
Jenny

Handwriting Tip: When you write the letter *n*, make sure it does not look like the letter *m*.

n

▶ **On each line, write the Spelling Word again.**

7. driving _____   8. hiding _____

9. giving _____   10. riding _____

SCHOOL-HOME CONNECTION Write the following words on slips of paper: *bake, dance, move, name,* and *smile.* Take turns choosing a word and spelling it when *-ed* and *-ing* are added. Remember to drop the *e* each time.

Harcourt

Name _____

▶ **Complete the sentences. Write a word from the suitcases on each line.**

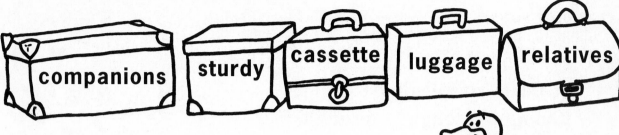

companions   sturdy   cassette   luggage   relatives

We will need to write to Grandma Duck and lots of other _____.

Let's pack our things in our _____.

Are these shoes _____ enough for hiking?

It's going to be a long ride, son! You may want to take your _____ player.

I'm bringing plenty of _____ along to keep me company!

 TRY THIS! Write about a trip you have taken. Use as many Vocabulary Words as you can.

 SCHOOL-HOME CONNECTION Ask your child to draw pictures about two of the Vocabulary Words and to label the pictures.

Just in Time **101**

Harcourt

Name _____

▶ **Complete the sentences. On the line, write the word that has the same vowel sound as *you* and that makes sense.**

1. My family hiked _____ part of Yellowstone Park last summer.
(thought   tough   through)

2. I'll bet _____ never been on a vacation like ours. **(yard   year   you've)**

3. _____ never believe all the things that went wrong.
(You'd   Yes   Yarn)

4. We were a tired, hungry _____ when we stopped for lunch. **(grape   gripe   group)**

5. That's when we found that we had left all our

_____ mix behind. **(sip   soup   sound)**

6. When we camped, it rained _____ the night.
(three   trip   throughout)

7. _____ can guess how we all looked and felt the next morning.
(Yam   You   Yell)

8. My parents said that camping was

only for children and _____.
(yarn   youths   yellow)

Harcourt

SCHOOL-HOME CONNECTION Ask your child to draw a picture of someone hiking through a forest and to label the picture, using the word *through*.

Name _____

▶ **Read the paragraphs. Think about the main idea. On the lines after each paragraph, write four details that support the main idea.**

Subways are a fast and easy way to travel around a city. The trains zip along underground much faster than a person can walk. Subways don't stop in traffic jams or for red lights. Subways can take you to most parts of the city, and they don't cost very much to ride.

1. _____

_____

2. _____

3. _____

4. _____

Would you like to take a trip on a boat? Huge ships carry thousands of people across the sea. Tiny sailboats sail near the shore. You can paddle a canoe on a river. Some people enjoy taking a rowboat out on a lake. As you can see, there are many kinds of boats to choose from.

5. _____

6. _____

7. _____

8. _____

Harcourt

SCHOOL-HOME CONNECTION Ask your child to write a paragraph about a boat ride. Remind him or her to write a sentence that tells the main idea and other sentences that give supporting details.

▶ **Read each paragraph. On each line, write the
sentence from the paragraph that tells the main idea.**

You can take a tour of the White House.
Also, see the place where money is printed.
Ride to the top of the Washington Monument
and enjoy the view of the city. Washington,
D.C., is a wonderful place for a vacation.

1. _____

_____

People of all ages can have fun on a vacation in New York
City. Everyone enjoys going up high in a skyscraper and looking
out over the city. A boat ride in the harbor is fun for all. There's
always something going on in Central Park, too.

2. _____

_____

Ride a swan boat in the Public Garden. Run and play on the
green grass of Boston Common. Have a picnic while you listen to
a concert. Then watch fireworks by the river. There's so much to
do in Boston in July!

3. _____

_____

Harcourt

SCHOOL-HOME CONNECTION Work with your child to write a
paragraph about a place you have visited or would like to visit.
Ask him or her to underline the main idea of the paragraph.

Name _____

▶ **Fill in the web to tell about the different ways to travel.**

How? on foot

Why? so you can stop and see the sights

How?

Why?

How?

Why?

You Can Travel

How?

Why?

How?

Why?

How?

Why?

What do you think is the best travel tip in the story?

_____

_____

Harcourt

SCHOOL-HOME CONNECTION Encourage your child to talk about some of the travel tips in the story "Dinosaurs Travel."

Name _____

▶ **Complete the sentences. On each line, write the word that makes sense and has the letter *c* and the sound at the beginning of *cent*.**

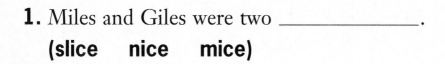

1. Miles and Giles were two _____.
 (slice   nice   mice)

2. They took a trip to the _____.
 (city   cereal   collar)

3. They found a place to stay near the _____
 of town. **(cents   center   car)**

4. The fast _____ of the city was a surprise
 to Miles and Giles. **(pact   pile   pace)**

5. They had to _____ across the streets
 to stay out of danger. **(rice   race   rose)**

6. A truck splashed mud on Miles's _____.
 (face   fact   fast)

7. "This is an interesting _____ to visit,"
 Giles said. **(town   place   nice)**

8. "Yes," agreed Miles, "but I don't want to come

 here _____!" **(toss   twice   while)**

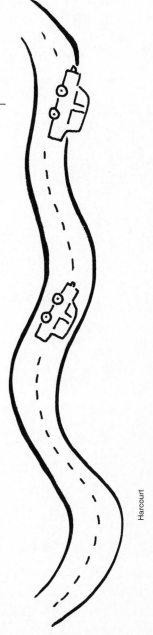

Harcourt

SCHOOL-HOME CONNECTION Work with your child to write a story
about mice running a race. Ask your child to circle each word in which
the letter *c* has the sound at the beginning of *cent*.

Name _____

▶ **Read the story. Find all the words that name ways to travel. Write these words on the lines.**

Lanny has to travel a long way to school. First, he rides his skateboard to the lake. He gets on a ferryboat to ride across the water. On the other side of the lake, a limousine meets Lanny and takes him to the airport. Then he boards a plane to fly to the city. There he takes a train to the station and then walks the rest of the way to school. By the time he gets to school, it's time to start home!

1. _____   2. _____

3. _____   4. _____

5. _____   6. _____

Harcourt

 TRY THIS! Write a sentence that tells how you travel to school. Draw a picture to go with your sentence.

SCHOOL-HOME CONNECTION Help your child make a list of words that name ways to travel. Ask him or her to write a sentence that uses one or more of the words.

Name _____

▶ **Read the words under each line. Choose the correct verb to finish the sentence. Write it on the line.**

1. Most people _____ by train.
   (comes   come)

2. It _____ into town at noon.
   (comes   come)

3. The trains _____ on time.
   (runs   run)

4. That man _____ on a bike.
   (came   come)

5. Some people _____ by bus.
   (comes   come)

6. The bus _____ on time, too.
   (runs   run)

7. Long ago, the bus _____ late.
   (ran   runs)

8. Sometimes people _____ for the train.
   (runs   run)

Harcourt

SCHOOL-HOME CONNECTION With your child, talk about a recent game you have played or a sports event you have seen. Encourage your child to use some of these verbs: come, comes, came; run, runs, ran.

Name _____

▶ **Complete the sentences. Write a Spelling Word on each line.**

circle	city	once	circus	nice	center

1. Everyone is happy when the _____ comes to town.

2. It stops in our _____ once a year.

3. Look at the elephants in the

   _____ ring.

4. The lion jumps through a _____ of fire.

5. _____, a clown shook my hand.

6. We always have a _____ time!

Handwriting Tip: When you write the letter *c*, do not make a full circle.

_____
C
_____

▶ **On each line, write a Spelling Word from a skateboard.**

 cents
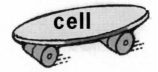 cell
 place
 since

7. _____   8. _____

9. _____   10. _____

SCHOOL-HOME CONNECTION With your child, brainstorm a list of boys' and girls' names that have a soft *c* sound, such as *Cindy, Lucy, Tracy, Vince,* and *Alice.*

Harcourt

Name _____

▶ **Finish the ad. Write a word from the box on each line.**

| soared | harbor | flock | swooping | glide |

Take a ride in one of Red's Ready Planes!

Have you ever **(1)** _____ across the sky? Have you ever seen a

(2) _____ of birds flying and wished you could fly, too? You can do it in one of Red's Ready Planes! You will

(3) _____ over the city. You will sail above the boats in the

(4) _____. Call Red today.

Soon you will be **(5)** _____ through the sky!

Harcourt

 TRY THIS! Imagine that you are a bird flying high in the sky. Write about what you see. Use as many Vocabulary Words as you can in your sentences.

 SCHOOL-HOME CONNECTION Ask your child to make a list of the Vocabulary Words and to number them. Write the numbers 1 through 5 on pieces of paper and turn them face down. Ask your child to choose a piece of paper and then to read the word from the list that has the same number.

Name _____

▶ **Read the sentences. Then answer
the questions.**

Poppy Pigeon left his nest because he was bored.

1. What is the cause? _____

2. What is the effect? _____

Poppy longed to fly over the buildings. He spread his wings and
took off.

3. What is the cause? _____

4. What is the effect? _____

Soon Poppy had to land on a roof because he was so tired.

5. What is the cause? _____

6. What is the effect? _____

Then a huge cat surprised Poppy. The bird flapped his wings
and sailed into the air.

7. What is the cause? _____

8. What is the effect? _____

_____

Harcourt

SCHOOL-HOME CONNECTION Talk with your child
about events that make both of you happy. Then ask your
child to write the cause and the effect of each event.

Just in Time **111**

Name _____

▶ **Complete the picture labels. Write a word from the box on each line.**

mice	face	circus	shoelace
ice	slice	cents	cereal

1. Come to the

_____!

2. two little

_____

3. the clown's

_____

4. a _____

that isn't tied

5. a _____ of

watermelon

6. a cube of

_____

7. a bowl of

_____

8. two _____

SCHOOL-HOME CONNECTION Ask your child to write the word *Circles* at the top of a sheet of paper. Draw a large circle and then work together to list in the circle as many things as you can that are in the shape of a circle.

Harcourt

Name _____

▶ **Fill in the web to show some of the things and places Rosalba and Abuela saw.**

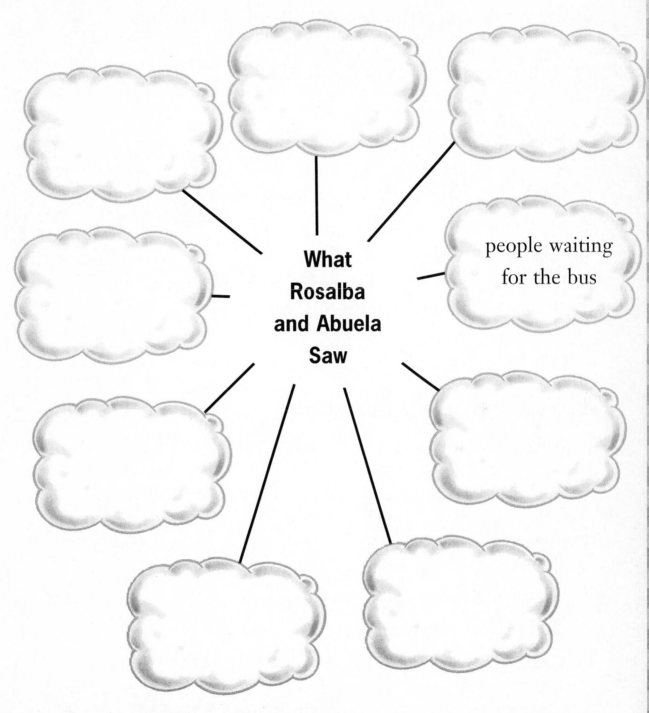

What Rosalba and Abuela Saw

people waiting for the bus

What is the story mostly about? _____

_____

SCHOOL-HOME CONNECTION Ask your child to tell you about the story "Abuela." Ask what adventures Rosalba and her grandmother have together.

Just in Time **113**

Harcourt

Name _____

▶ **Read the sentences. Add an ending from the box to each word in ( ). Make a new word that makes sense in the sentence. Write the new word on the line.**

ful	ly	ness

1. Everyone likes Chirpy because he sings

   (joy) _____ songs.

2. He sits in the tree and sings

   (loud) _____ every morning.

3. "If I'm feeling sad, Chirpy makes my

   (sad) _____ go away!" Mrs. Pearson says.

4. Chirpy is known for his **(gentle)** _____, too.

5. If you hold out a slice of bread, Chirpy will fly down and

   land **(quiet)** _____ on your arm.

6. Chirpy is very **(play)** _____ sometimes.

7. He swoops down and **(careful)** _____ pecks
   the back of a sleeping dog.

8. What a surprise the dog has when it feels the

   (sharp) _____ of Chirpy's beak!

SCHOOL-HOME CONNECTION With your child, make a list of words that end with -ful, -ly, and -ness. Encourage your child to tell you what each word means.

Harcourt

Name _____

▶ **Read the paragraph. Choose the word that belongs in each space. Fill in the circle next to your choice.**

Jim was **(1)** _____ that he would enjoy his first plane ride. With his seat belt pulled **(2)** _____ around him, Jim was ready for take-off. The jet engine noise grew louder, and **(3)** _____ the plane rose into the sky. As the plane flew through the **(4)** _____, Jim seemed to be riding on an enormous bird. He saw the clouds **(5)** _____ passing by. When Jim got sleepy, the **(6)** _____ flight attendant brought him a pillow.

1 ⬭ hope
⬭ hopeful
⬭ hopefulness
⬭ hoped

2 ⬭ snugly
⬭ snuggle
⬭ snug
⬭ snugness

3 ⬭ darkness
⬭ darkly
⬭ darken
⬭ darkening

4 ⬭ slowness
⬭ slow
⬭ slowing
⬭ slowly

5 ⬭ quickness
⬭ quicker
⬭ quickly
⬭ quick

6 ⬭ helpful
⬭ helping
⬭ help
⬭ helped

Harcourt

Name _____

▶ **Read the Spanish words and their meanings.**
Answer the questions by writing a correct
Spanish word on each line.

Spanish Word	Meaning
abuela	grandmother
banana	a fruit
burro	a donkey
coyote	an animal in the dog family
mango	a fruit
papaya	a fruit
patio	an outdoor room of a home
rodeo	a roping and riding contest

Which three words name kinds of fruit?

1. _____ 2. _____ 3. _____

Which word can mean "mother's mother"? 4. _____

What animal can carry riders and packs? 5. _____

What animal howls and is not tame? 6. _____

Which word means a room to sit in outdoors? 7. _____

Where do cowhands show off their skills? 8. _____

Harcourt

SCHOOL-HOME CONNECTION Ask your child to
write several sentences that include Spanish words
that are used in English.

Name _____

▶ **Complete the sentences. Write a word from the box on each line.**

| go | goes | went | do | does | did |

1. The bus _____ fast now.

2. It _____ slowly last week.

3. The driver _____ a good job last week.

4. She _____ a good job now, too.

5. Now many people _____ on bus trips.

6. Last year one driver _____ the wrong way.

7. He _____ not do a good job last year.

8. All the drivers _____ their best now.

TRY THIS! Talk with a partner. Take turns telling about special places you have gone and special things you have done. Use the verbs *go, goes, went* and *do, does, did*.

Harcourt

SCHOOL-HOME CONNECTION Ask your child these questions: Where did you go today? What did you do there? Encourage your child to use the verbs *went* and *did* when answering.

Name _____

▶ Complete each sentence with three words that
rhyme. Write a Spelling Word from the box on each line.

tried	skies	cried	flies	cries	dried

The baby **(1)** _____ while

her mother **(2)** _____ her off

and **(3)** _____ to rock her to sleep.

The little bird **(4)** _____ while

the mother bird **(5)** _____

to faraway **(6)** _____.

Handwriting Tip: When you write, make your letters
smooth and even. They should not be too light or too dark.

too light   too dark   just right

ladies   **ladies**   ladies

▶ On each line, write a Spelling Word from the box.

puppies	flying	dries	ladies

7. _____   **8.** _____

9. _____   **10.** _____

SCHOOL-HOME CONNECTION With your child, add -es to the following
words: *country, company, family, study,* and *worry.* Remember to change
the *y* to *i* first. Then make up a sentence using each word.

Harcourt

▶ **Finish the story. Write a word from the box on
each line.**

| spectators | heroine | stood |
| feat | refused | hospitality |

A noise startled Milly. Three young cats had fallen into the river
and were crying for help. Milly pulled them out. "Milly is our

(1) _____!" all the **(2)** _____said.
"She saved Jack and his brothers!"

Jack told about Milly's **(3)** _____.
"She saved three of us in one day. That tops a record that has

(4) _____ for years," he said. Mrs. Cat
gave a party for Milly. Milly thanked Mrs. Cat for her

(5) _____. She **(6)** _____ to accept
any more attention.

"I was just helping my friends," she said.

SCHOOL-HOME CONNECTION Ask your child to draw a picture of an
event that many spectators watch. Then ask your child to write a sentence about the picture, using at least one Vocabulary Word.

Harcourt

Name _____

▶ **Finish the story. Add the suffix *-ful, -ly,* or**
-ness **to the word in ( ) to make a new word. Write the new**
word on the line.

ful	ly	ness

1. In his imagination, Kareem flew his plane through

the _____. **(dark)**

2. The little plane _____ rose higher
and higher. **(slow)**

3. Kareem hardly felt the _____ of
the night. **(cold)**

4. He was _____ for his warm
jacket. **(thank)**

5. "I'm glad I have this _____ map,"
he said. **(use)**

6. "It will help me find my way _____."
(correct)

7. Soon Kareem had gone _____
around the earth. **(complete)**

8. "That trip went _____!" he said. **(perfect)**

SCHOOL-HOME CONNECTION Ask your child to write the words
helpful and *harmful* at the top of a sheet of paper as column headings.
Work together to list things that belong in each column.

Harcourt

Name _____

▶ **Read the sentences about Lincoln Beachey, a pilot who lived at about the same time as Ruth Law. Then write the part of the sentence that tells the cause and the part that tells the effect.**

Since Lincoln Beachey loved flying, he often went up in balloons.

1. Cause: _____

2. Effect: _____

By 1910 balloons were not as popular, so Beachey learned to fly airplanes.

3. Cause: _____

4. Effect: _____

Beachey crashed many planes because he didn't know much about flying airplanes.

5. Cause: _____

6. Effect: _____

Soon he learned to do fancy tricks in the air, so people paid money to see him fly.

7. Cause: _____

8. Effect: _____

Harcourt

SCHOOL-HOME CONNECTION Work with your child to write a story about an airplane adventure. Help him or her to include several sentences that tell the causes of events and their effects.

Name _____

▶ **Complete the cause-and-effect chart to retell
the story.**

CAUSE	EFFECT
Ruth wanted to get used to cold weather.	She slept in a tent on a hotel roof.
Ruth's plane was too heavy with a second gas tank.	
	She had to make an emergency landing.
Ruth could not read her flight instruments in the dark.	
Ruth set a nonstop cross-country flying record.	

How do you think Ruth Law felt at the end of her flight?

_____

SCHOOL-HOME CONNECTION Ask your child to share what
he or she learned from the story "Ruth Law Thrills a Nation."
Ask what problems Ruth Law had when she flew to New York.

Harcourt

Name _____

Ruth Law Thrills
a Nation

Vowel Variants:
/o͞o/oo and
/o͝o/oo, ou

▶ **Complete the sentences. On each line, write the word that makes sense and has the same vowel sound as *foot* or *food*.**

1. I read about old airplanes in a library _____.
    (bake   book   took)

2. They were made of light _____. **(woke   wade   wood)**

3. There was _____ for only one pilot.
    (race   room   look)

4. Those old planes _____ not fly very far.
    (would   wound   wall)

5. They _____ get only a few feet up into the air.
    (cold   cook   could)

6. The ride was not very _____.
    (smooth   shall   tooth)

7. _____ they had to land. **(same   sing   soon)**

8. I'm glad we have _____ planes to ride in now.
    (gold   good   gate)

TRY THIS! Write a sentence with the words *should* and *cool*. Circle the letters that stand for the vowel sound in *foot* or the vowel sound in *food*.

SCHOOL-HOME CONNECTION Help your child trace his or her foot on a sheet of paper. Then ask your child to fill the tracing with words that have the same vowel sound as *foot*.

Harcourt

Name _____

▶ **Look at each picture and read the sentences
beside it. On the line, write the sentence in which the
underlined word has the same meaning it
has in the picture.**

It was Lou's dream to <u>fly</u> his own plane.
A <u>fly</u> landed in my bowl of soup.

1. _____

Cindy will <u>pitch</u> the big game for our team.
Look at that plane dip and <u>pitch</u> in the wind!

2. _____

The soaring birds looked <u>striking</u> against the sunset.
Dad is <u>striking</u> the nail with the hammer.

3. _____

I wore a cowboy <u>tie</u> to the rodeo.
I'm going to <u>tie</u> a tail onto my kite.

4. _____

The drummer played a fast <u>beat</u>.
Ellen <u>beat</u> all the other runners in the race.

5. _____

Harcourt

SCHOOL-HOME CONNECTION Challenge your child to
draw pictures that show two meanings of the word *foot*.
Ask him or her to write a sentence about each picture.

Name _____

▶ **Complete the sentences. Write a helping verb on each line.**

1. We _____ not yet met the pilot.

2. She _____ flown on many trips.

3. _____ you ever been in a plane?

4. Mr. Wicks _____ never taken a plane ride.

5. He _____ gone to the airport many times.

6. I _____ watched many planes, too.

7. A big plane _____ just landed.

8. We _____ always liked planes.

 TRY THIS! Write three sentences about things you and your friends have done in the past. Use a helping verb and a main verb in each sentence. Draw a picture to go with your sentences.

SCHOOL-HOME CONNECTION Ask your child to explain helping verbs. Then have your child make up a sentence with the helping verb *has*, *have*, or *had*.

Just in Time **125**

Harcourt

Name _____

▶ **Match the Spelling Words to the picture clues.**
Write a Spelling Word from the box on each line.

cook	books	foot	stood	woods	hook

1. _____

2. _____

3. _____

4. _____

5. _____

6. _____

Handwriting Tip: Write all letters so that they sit on the bottom line.

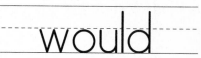

would

▶ **Write a Spelling Word from the cloud on each line.**

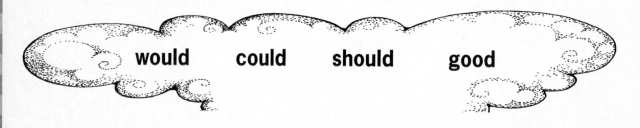

would   could   should   good

7. _____   8. _____

9. _____   10. _____

126 Just in Time

SCHOOL-HOME CONNECTION With your child, make a list of objects around your home that have the ŏŏ sound in their names, such as *hooks* and *books*.

Harcourt

Name _____

▶ **Complete the sentences. Write a word from
the box on each line.**

reflects	dangerous	guide	assembled
surface		lightning	intense

1. Dee _____ her Zip Ship from a kit.

2. She was sure that a trip in her brand-new ship would not

be _____ at all.

3. "I won't need a _____ if I just use the map,"
she said.

4. Dee wanted to stay away from the _____
heat of the sun.

5. How exciting it was to soar over the rocky

_____ of the moon!

6. Dee could see how the moon

_____ the sun's light.

7. "My ship zips around as fast as

_____!" she said.

Harcourt

SCHOOL-HOME CONNECTION Have your child write each
Vocabulary Word on a separate piece of paper. Take turns
with your child, choosing a word and reading it aloud.

Name _____

▶ **Finish the story. Write a word from the box on each line.**

soon	would	good-bye	could
school	took	shook	stood

Blast Off to the Moon

I **(1)** _____ hardly wait for my first ride in a spaceship! "Welcome aboard!" said the pilot as she

(2) _____ my hand. "We will be leaving

(3) _____," she told me. I said **(4)** _____ to

my mom and dad. They **(5)** _____ on the ground and

waved while I **(6)** _____ my seat inside the spaceship.

In only three days I **(7)** _____ be walking on the

moon. "Just wait until I tell my friends at **(8)** _____ about this!" I said.

 TRY THIS! Write a story about a ride on a spaceship. Use as many words from the box as you can.

 SCHOOL-HOME CONNECTION Ask your child to write each of the words from the box. Then ask him or her to point out the letters that stand for the vowel sound in *cool* and for the vowel sound in *book*.

128 Just in Time

Harcourt

Name _____

▶ **Solve the riddles. Write a word from the box on each line.**

face	circle	cymbal	circus	mice
center	race	cereal	city	cents

1. People eat it along with milk. It's _____.

2. It's more than one mouse. It's _____.

3. Your eyes and nose are on it. It's your _____.

4. Ten of these make one dime. They are _____.

5. It has a round shape. It's a _____.

6. It's the spot in the middle. It's the _____.

7. This goes "Crash!" when the drummer hits it.

It's a _____.

8. It's a very big town. It's a _____.

9. Run fast, and you may win one of these.

It's a _____.

10. You'll find clowns and elephants here.

It's a _____.

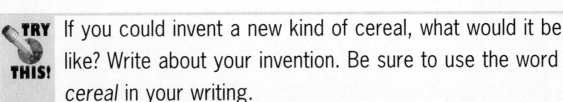

Harcourt

TRY THIS! If you could invent a new kind of cereal, what would it be like? Write about your invention. Be sure to use the word *cereal* in your writing.

SCHOOL-HOME CONNECTION Ask your child to draw a picture of a city and label it, using the word *city*. Then ask him or her to point out the letter that stands for the sound at the beginning of *center*.

Name _____

▶ **Complete the sentences. Add a suffix from the
box to each word in ( ). Write the new word on the line.**

ful	ly	ness

1. Terry stepped _____ out of his spaceship.
(brave)

2. There was a strange _____ in the air. **(still)**

3. Very _____, Terry took a few steps. **(slow)**

4. "I wonder if there is anything _____ on this
planet," he said. **(use)**

5. _____ he saw a cloud of dust not far away.
(Sudden)

6. "What could that be?" Terry said in a _____
voice. **(fear)**

7. In the _____ it was hard to see what was
coming over the hill. **(dark)**

8. "I hope whatever lives on this planet is _____,"
he thought. **(friend)**

 **TRY
THIS!** Write what you think will happen next in this story. Use as
many words as you can that end with *-ful*, *-ly*, and *-ness*.

 SCHOOL-HOME CONNECTION Talk with your child about things that
are done quietly and things that are done loudly. Ask him or her to list
them on a sheet of paper under the headings *quietly* and *loudly*.

Harcourt

Name _____

▶ Before you read "Postcards from Pluto," fill in the first two parts of this K-W-L chart. Write what you know and what you want to know. After you read the story, write what you learned.

Solar System

K	W	L
What I **K**now	What I **W**ant to Know	What I **L**earned

Write a sentence about our solar system.

_____

_____

SCHOOL-HOME CONNECTION Encourage your child to share some facts he or she learned from the story "Postcards from Pluto."

Name _____

▶ **Complete the sentences. Write a word from the box on each line.**

straw	caught	laundry	launch
saw	fault	dawn	taught

1. I've been awake since before ___dawn___.

2. I can sip this milk through a ___straw___.

3. I've ___caught___ a cold!

4. How will we wash our ___laundry___?

5. Has anyone ___taught___ you how to fly this thing?

6. It's my ___fault___ we forgot the map of Pluto.

7. I know I ___saw___ a new planet!

8. Let's watch a replay of our ___launch___ on TV!

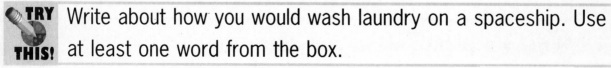

TRY THIS! Write about how you would wash laundry on a spaceship. Use at least one word from the box.

SCHOOL-HOME CONNECTION Have your child write three sentences about things he or she has been taught to do. Ask your child to use the word *taught* in each sentence.

Harcourt

Name _____

▶ **Solve the riddles. Write a word from the box on each line.**

| galaxy | orbit | star | asteroid |
| crater | planet | comet | rotate |

1. This word means "to spin." What is it?

   to _____

2. This is a very big group of stars. What is it?

   a _____

3. What's a name for a space rock?

   an _____

4. This word means "to travel around." What is it?

   to _____

5. It gives off heat and light. What is it?

   a _____

6. What's a hole made by an asteroid?

   a _____

7. This orbits a star. What is it?

   a _____

8. This is made of frozen gas and dust. What is it?

   a _____

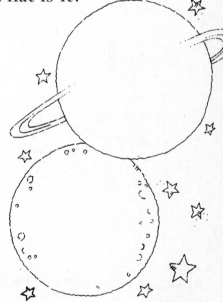

SCHOOL-HOME CONNECTION Have your child draw a picture of the solar system. Ask him or her to label the picture.

Harcourt

Name _____

▶ **Complete the sentences. On each line, write a contraction of the two words in ( ).**

1. I _____ get a postcard from Teri. **(did not)**

2. She _____ on the trip. **(was not)**

3. She _____ go after all. **(could not)**

4. That _____ fair! **(is not)**

5. I _____ heard from Ross. **(have not)**

6. You _____ wait for his
   card. **(should not)**

7. He _____ send postcards. **(does not)**

8. I _____ worry about it. **(would not)**

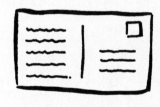

TRY THIS! Write three sentences you might say when you don't want to do something. Use a different contraction in each sentence.

SCHOOL-HOME CONNECTION Ask your child to explain what a contraction is. Then have your child write three contractions, such as *isn't, don't,* and *couldn't.* Ask what two words are written together in each contraction and what mark is used in place of the missing letters.

Harcourt

Name _____

▶ **Finish the story. Write a Spelling Word from
the box on each line.**

| cause | thought | small | ball | cough | August | fall |

A Short Trip

In **(1)** ___August___, my family took a trip before I went

back to school in the **(2)** ___fall___. My parents rented a

(3) ___small___ car. We **(4)** ___thought___ we would

be gone for two weeks. Then my little brother got a bad

(5) ___cough___. We came home early. The doctor said the

(6) ___cause___ was being away from home. That was fine

with me. I like playing **(7)** ___ball___ more than riding in
a car.

Handwriting Tip: When you write
the letter *w*, make sure it does not look
like the letter *v*.

W   V

▶ **On each line, write the Spelling Word again.**

8. jaw ___jaw___   9. saw ___saw___   10. draw ___draw___

SCHOOL-HOME CONNECTION Have your child write a short
story using four Spelling Words. Talk with your child about the
letters that make the /ô/ sound in each of those words.

Just in Time **135**

Harcourt

Skills and Strategies Index